Does My Dog Need Prozac?

Musings and sound advice
on living with a shy, anxious,
fearful or reactive dog.

By Debbie Jacobs CPDT-KA, CAP2

Does My Dog Need Prozac?

Visit fearfuldogs.com

Published by Corner Dog Press in Guilford, Vermont
cornerdogpress.com

Published June 2014 — First printing

Printed in the USA

ISBN 978-0-9888841-2-0

Illustrations by Leslie Swieck

Cover and book design by www.flocksholmdesign.com

For all the dogs who are struggling to find a life worth living,
and for those of you joining them on that journey.

Enjoy the journey!

CONTENTS

PREFACE

If you picked up this book because you are wondering if your dog would benefit from medications it is probably time to contact your veterinarian or a veterinarian behaviorist to discuss the options. As yet there are no magic cures to treat dogs suffering from fears, phobias and anxieties, but the use of behavioral medications has proven to be an important component in the treatment and rehabilitation of many of these dogs. Delaying treatment may be prolonging a dog's suffering and contribute to a degradation in behavior that will only be more challenging, or impossible, to address as time goes by.

Your next call should be to a trainer who understands the impact fear has on a dog's behavior, and who is skilled in creating desensitization and counter-conditioning protocols to help your dog feel more comfortable in their world. They should be trained in the use of positive reinforcement to teach dogs new behaviors and they should refrain from using corrections or pieces of equipment that are designed to hurt, scare or threaten a dog. An educated trainer should be able to tell you why punishment works to change behavior and what the possible risks are of using it.

Fearful, anxious and phobic dogs and those of us caring for them are a vulnerable population. We are at risk of falling for promises of quick fixes, regardless of there being solid evidence supporting their success. These fixes may include the use of dietary calming aids or inhumane and ultimately ineffective training methods. Both money and time are wasted while our dogs continue to suffer.

Helping my own dog move out of a corner and into the world he was dropped into has been among the most challenging, and rewarding efforts in my life. I could not have done it on my own and am grateful for the shoulders offered to me to stand on in order to reach goals with him. Far better minds than my own have been devoted to creating effective and ethical methods for giving our dogs the skills they need to feel safe in their lives. I hesitate listing them for fear of leaving anyone out. I want to thank every trainer, behaviorist, veterinarian, and educator who is providing force-free, science-based information and resources to those of us on the frontlines living and working with a fearful dog. Your work is important and has been of value to many. Carry on, please.

Debbie Jacobs CPDT-KA, CAP2
Guilford VT
May 2104

HOW TO BE A FRIEND
TO A FEARFUL DOG

Posted December 11, 2008

Since Sunny landed in our living room and settled into the corner, my *shy-dog radar* seems to have been fine-tuned. At a pet shop recently, a young woman was browsing the dog treat section; her young, black and white dog was doing the same. When I turned to speak to the woman, making small talk about kids in candy stores, her dog took one look at me, ducked his head, and stepped back, his eyes locked on my face. I'd seen that look enough to know that I should not return the stare and immediately turned my head. The dog resumed his sniffing of the various dried, animal body parts available to him.

"A bit shy, isn't he?", I remarked.

"Oh, he scares himself," his owner replied, "Someone looks at him and he looks back and gets scared and starts barking."

I tried to follow her line of reasoning (he scares himself?), but knew better than to spend too much energy on the task. The list of explanations that owners make regarding why their fearful dog behaves the way he does and why the owner responds the way s/he does is long, and might be funny except that dogs are suffering.

Researchers and scientists agree that dogs experience the emotion of fear. Not only is fear biologically advantageous (do something or die), dogs that are afraid behave in ways that look a lot like the ways humans behave when we're afraid. We startle, we cringe, we turn away, we run, we scream, we shake— you get the picture.

When I was seven years old I jumped off of a high diving board for the first time. My family was on holiday and the hotel we were staying at had a pool. I watched other kids climb up the ladder, walk out to the edge of the board, leap off into space, and plunge into the water below. My father asked me if I wanted to try it. Together we climbed up the ladder and as soon as I got to the top, I turned and headed back down, weaving past the line of kids following us up for their turn. My father did not force me to continue.

Back in the pool I watched the other children jumping off and again my father encouraged me to give it a try. This time he said he'd stay in the pool and come to get me after I splashed down. For some reason this made me feel more inclined to try it, so again I climbed the ladder, got to the top, walked out to the end of the board, and leapt off, keeping my eyes on my father in the water below. I wasn't in the water for more than a few seconds before I felt his hands on me, giving me support while I caught my breath from the excitement of it all. From that day on I have been a fan of jumping off high diving boards, rope swings, boats, ledges—you name it—so long as I'm going to land in deep water.

I don't share this story just to fill you in on my personal recreation habits or my childhood, but because it is full of lessons on how to work with a fearful dog. Two important components of this scenario are applicable to the work we do with our scared dogs.

1. I had a trusting relationship with my father.

2. I had the skills needed to succeed at the task.

The person encouraging me to do something that scared me was my father. I trusted him. If a stranger had offered to take my hand and lead me up that ladder, I would have been wide-eyed in terror; I might have even reacted the same way if it was my older brother. My father said I'd be alright and I believed him. He was not in the habit of putting me in dangerous situations, and I trusted his ability to protect me from anything, in the way that only little girls can (and probably should) feel about their fathers. He had taught me how to swim and for years I had been jumping off the docks and piers a few feet above the surface of the lake where we spent our summers. I had the skills and experience to climb that ladder and launch myself into the deep end of a pool, I just hadn't done it before.

Stand 6 month-old-babies on their feet and let go of them and they don't start walking, they fall down. Their brains have not developed the intricate and remarkable circuitry to control their movement and their bodies don't have the physical strength. Someday though they'll be able to, unless they never get the chance to practice (or have a physical or mental disability).

Many dogs, especially puppy-mill and pet-shop dogs, don't get the chance to practice the skills necessary in order for them to be able to handle the social interactions, the delicate balance of acting and reacting, that a pet owner expects of them. Some of them, with gentle guidance and coaching in the hands of someone they trust, will be able to catch up and learn to enjoy being around the things that once made them uncomfortable (or flat out horrified them), but others will not, not ever. The damage has been done, there's no making up or repairing some brain development. All may not be lost, but for the average pet owner a dog like this is never going to be the dog of their dreams (unless they've dreamt of having a dog that prefers to live in the closet).

We humans tend to be an impatient bunch and rather than proceeding slowly with our dogs, we keep trying to make them stand up when all that happens is that they topple over, again and again. Some dogs will begin to actively resist our efforts (growling or snapping) others will give up. Though they may comply with what they are being forced to do, they are not enjoying it. They are establishing negative associations with the experience, and the human forcing them into it.

It is possible to change how a dog feels and behaves around the things that scare them. Even a dog that isn't exactly the dog of someone's dreams can have a good life and provide their owner with companionship and joy. Making this happen usually means changing how we think about our scared dogs. It means questioning the things we've been told about dogs and how they learn new skills. It means that we stop tossing them off the high board and into the deep end and expect them to thank us for it.

"

WHEN WE EXPERIENCE RESISTANCE
FROM OUR DOGS, IT GIVES US THE OPPORTUNITY
TO CONSIDER WHAT THEIR PREFERENCE MIGHT BE.
WE MAY NOT KNOW WITH 100% CERTAINTY
WHY THEY ARE BEHAVING THE WAY THEY ARE,
BUT WE CAN KNOW WHY WE CHOOSE
TO RESPOND TO THEM THE WAY WE DO.

OUR BIG BRAINS ALLOW US TO DECIDE
WHETHER BEING ANGRY, FRUSTRATED OR SCARED
JUSTIFIES RESPONDING WITH FORCE OR COERCION.
AND WHETHER OUR RESPONSE IS GOING
TO RESOLVE OUR CONFLICT IN A MANNER
WHICH WILL HELP IMPROVE RATHER THAN
CONTRIBUTE TO THE DETERIORATION
OF OUR RELATIONSHIP.

"

BE A BETTER TRAINER
NOT A STRONGER LEADER

Posted December 18, 2008

At an agility trial over the weekend, I met a young woman who ran a rescue organization. She was at the event to run her own dog, a small breed mix that should be auditioning for the next Disney film it was so darn cute. Between runs we met in the parking lot; she had a different dog, a pom/chi mix, that was visibly nervous. It was relinquished by the owners because it had begun to show aggression toward the husband of the couple that had him. It was young and appeared to have a decent shot at becoming a good pet for someone.

I chatted with the woman a bit and mentioned that it was lucky that the dog was given up at such a young age; too often people will tolerate behaviors from small dogs that they never would from a bigger dog, until the day they can't tolerate them. By then the dog has had years of practicing an inappropriate behavior and ends up being impossible to rehome.

"Yes," the woman agreed, "Why treat a small dog differently than a big dog?"

The woman told me that she was doing the "leadership thing" with the dog and had not had any problems with the dog. At that point I could only guess what this "leadership thing" technique looked like, but I was soon to see it in action.

Walking back into the building the small dog came nose to nose with another dog and began to growl and back away from it. The woman bent down, grabbed the small dog and shoved it toward the other dog saying, "You'll deal with it and be fine, that's how you'll learn." I stopped, stared, and my jaw dropped. Imagine grabbing your growling pittie or German Shepherd and pushing it toward another dog that it was afraid of. Just because you can do something to a dog doesn't mean you should.

5

There is no doubt in my mind that the small dog had no understanding that it was to learn that other dogs were not to be feared, or that it actually came to that conclusion. I will only surmise on a few lessons the dog did learn. Only time and the dog's behavior will tell how that education affected the dog.

He might have learned:

People are not to be trusted. The next time someone grabs you it might be a good idea to try to prevent that from happening.

Growling and backing away from something that scares you only makes you land in its face; try something else next time, biting might work or just give up and shut down.

Places where there are other dogs are where bad things happen.

The woman with this dog obviously cares about dogs and the animals that live with her may be among the fortunate ones on the planet. But even skilled handlers still hold on to misconceptions about how dogs learn new behaviors and how you change the associations they have with things that scare them.

It's not about learning to be a better leader; it's about learning to be a better trainer.

BAD ADVICE

Posted December 27, 2008

Advising someone with a fearful or shy dog to expose their dog to whatever induces fear in him without encouraging owners to have an understanding of thresholds, counterconditioning, and desensitization is irresponsible.

Every dog is different and just because someone has had success in improving fear-based behaviors with their dog (or even a number of dogs), using techniques such as flooding or *exposure*, does not mean that it is appropriate for many dogs. Forcing a dog to interact with or experience things that scare it can cause a dog to become more sensitive to their triggers (the things that scare them), and may increase their level of fear toward them and could cause them to behave aggressively.

I happen to enjoy swimming, as do many members of my family. The children all learned to swim at young ages and are comfortable and safe in deep water. It would be irresponsible for me to encourage any child or adult to jump into deep water or dive into ocean waves if I am not familiar with their swimming ability. Neither should I advise parents to allow their child to be unsupervised around bodies of water until they were certain that their child had the necessary skills to be safe in those situations.

Yet people routinely advise owners of fearful dogs to ignore their dog's fears and put the dog in situations in which the dog does not have the skills to be safe and comfortable. This advice may be well meaning but, without seeing a dog, the safest course of action for any owner of a scared dog acknowledges the dog's fears and follows a course of management and training that includes counterconditioning and desensitization. As well intentioned as the givers of advice to use flooding or exposure may be, they are often not there to help owners and dogs who find themselves in over their heads and struggling.

WHAT IS LEARNED HELPLESSNESS?

Posted January 14, 2009

TV's *The Dog Whisperer* has made "learned helplessness" all the rage. There is no question that it is possible to get behaviors from dogs using a variety of different techniques. If you stood over your kid with a mallet and threatened him with violence if he didn't do his homework, you may get the homework done, but at what cost? It is that cost that has gone unnoticed by Cesar Millan and his many advocates when the threat of punishment, intimidation, or pain is used to change behaviors in dogs. Dogs who are bullied into behaving certain ways may behave that way so long as the abuser is present, so a *resource guarder* may allow Dad to take his bones away but junior gets bitten. It's not about being alpha or being the pack leader; it's about changing how a dog perceives having its food and toys handled by people, and that takes training, not bullying.

Worse then just choosing to selectively comply with particular behavior requests is a dog that no longer makes a choice. This is called learned helplessness and the laboratory studies done to define and describe this condition are pretty miserable to read. A dog was subjected to electrical shocks on the floor while in a room with a low divider that had an area on the other side where no shocks were administered. Some dogs were allowed to jump over the divider to escape the shocks, while others were not. The dogs that were not allowed to jump over the divider after repeatedly being shocked stopped trying to escape the shocks, even when the opportunity for escape was offered to them. They basically gave up trying to help themselves!

So what does this have to do with television's *Dog Whisperer*? Ever watch an episode in which a dog was repeatedly forced to walk on a particular surface, be near something, or otherwise be made to deal with whatever scared it? Eventually the dog stops resisting and complies and everyone smiles and feels warm and fuzzy cause the dog has been cured. In most cases the dog is not feeling warm and fuzzy and has not learned to not be afraid of what is scaring it; it has just learned to stop trying to make the terror go away. This may be enough for many dog owners, but it does nothing to create or maintain a positive, trusting relationship with a dog, and has not given the dog (or owner) any new skills in how to manage challenging situations.

I love watching dogs perform tricks, run agility courses, leap for frisbees, fling themselves off docks to chase a tennis ball, or sit in front of a toddler with a paw raised and an expectant look on their face as they mug for a treat. A dog performs these behaviors not only because he was trained to, but because the behaviors are fun and rewarding to him. These behaviors were learned by the dog. Dogs can learn all kinds of new behaviors to replace inappropriate ones, but not if they've given up believing that their behavior can positively effect their experience.

ATTITUDES ABOUT TRAINING

Posted February 1, 2009

I found a copy of one of William Koehler's training books in a local used bookstore. He was a trainer that worked in Hollywood, training dogs for films that I watched as a child. Had I known his training techniques then, I probably would have cried before the dog got caught in a well or suffered some other fate that was geared to jerking the tears out of a 9-year-old's eyes.

The list of training aids prescribed by Mr. Koehler includes a variety of choke chains and, should an owner be inclined to molly-coddle their dog, he clearly advises the use of a piece of hose or a folded-up newspaper. (I suppose the newspaper idea caught on as the kinder corrective measure.) But lest I forget, there's the leather strap or belt used to hit a dog hard—and I kid you not.

Koehler's willingness to use brute force to manage dogs is matched by his contempt for anyone that disagreed with his methods, the "wincers" as he called them—a tidbit-tossing group of naive dog handlers. But, as can be possible in anything, there are grains of truth and reason in his initial assertion in the book that in order to train a dog you need to get its attention. Koehler's method of training gets a dog's attention through a series of exercises that teach the dog that not paying attention hurts.

While training has changed over the decades, and since this is the only book of Koehler's that I've read (he died in 1993), I don't know if he recanted on any of his beliefs about how best to handle a dog. But what has not changed over the decades for many trainers is the attitude about the relationship people have with their dogs.

Koehler describes a dog that avoids his owner's attempts to get a hold of him as competitive, as opposed to untrained, playful, or even scared. There is no recognition that dogs may have rich and varied interests that don't always coincide with their owner's goals—a very different way of looking at inappropriate behaviors. A dog that is behaving aggressively because of fear is asking for something very different than a dog that is behaving aggressively and is not afraid; and your feelings about the behavior should reflect this difference. A child crying at the checkout counter at the grocery store because they can't have a pack of bubble gum is very different from a child crying because their finger is caught in the door. Hopefully your impatience with the behavior is reserved for the former.

The beauty of using positive reinforcement when training a dog is that it does not matter why the dog is behaving aggressively, the training is not likely to make the behavior worse by scaring a fearful dog or making an already confident, angry dog more upset. It reminds me of the theme common in films: the protagonist's motives are misunderstood, they are punished, but at the end they are redeemed, seen for the hero they truly are. If only a fearful dog's story could be condensed into 90 minutes.

Today there are popular trainers who persist in simplifying our relationship with our dogs into that of leader and follower. All behavioral indiscretions on the part of our dogs are the result of a lack of leadership by owners or sloppy leadership; the dogs are grateful when their owners step up to the plate and start taking charge. Advocates of the "pack leader" theory of dog training will point to results, much the same way that William Koehler does in his training book. The end justifies the means as they say. But does it? Getting a scared dog to behave a certain way because it is too frightened to do otherwise hardly sounds like a success to me.

In a telling clip of Cesar Millan working with a fearful American Eskimo dog, the caged dog snarls and snaps when approached—a tactic which has probably worked in the past to keep people away from it, which is the point of the behavior. A trapped dog has few choices. Unyielding to the display, Cesar approaches the cage and towers over the dog who some would say "calms" down, though I doubt the dog is feeling calm at all; freezing or the lack of movement does not mean that a dog is feeling good about the situation. Once leashed up and outside the cage, the dog raises a paw which Cesar describes as a predatory behavior which is an indication that he needs to continue to be wary of the dog.

I don't disagree on the latter, but paw raises have a multitude of meanings for dogs (many of which we may not fully understand), and, while a paw raise may indicate predatory intentions if the dog is stalking the family cat, it is often seen as an appeasement gesture, a sign of indecision, or as Turid Rugaas would describe a "calming signal"—not surprising coming from a dog that has been threatened. Just because physical force is not used on a dog, it is implied when one uses their size and body posturing to subdue them. The fact that the gun pointed at your head is not loaded probably won't make any difference to you if you're not aware of the fact or of the wielder's intent; it's probably best to go along with their demands.

"

ONE OF THE PRIMARY GOALS WE SHOULD HAVE
IN MIND FOR OUR FEARFUL DOGS IS
TO NEVER PUT THEM IN SITUATIONS
IN WHICH THEY FEEL THE NEED TO BEHAVE
IN AN AGGRESSIVE MANNER OR ESCALATE
ANY AGGRESSION THEY ARE ALREADY DISPLAYING.

WE CAN LET OUR DOGS SAY, "NO," AND THEN,
USING APPROPRIATE REWARD-BASED TRAINING
TECHNIQUES GET THEM TO SAY, "SURE, GO FOR IT."
DON'T BUY INTO THE IDEA THAT THERE ARE SOME
DOGS WHO CAN ONLY COME TO AN AGREEMENT
WITH US IF WE PROVE TO THEM WE ARE WILLING
TO HURT, THREATEN, OR BULLY THEM.

"

WHAT'S YOUR THEORY?

Posted February 3, 2009

I've been reading a lot of dog training books lately and many trainers provide readers with the reasons their method of training dogs works or makes sense. More often than not it has something to do with wolves, pack behavior, prey drive, alpha animals, what's "natural," etc. Statements are made about what dogs want or need. Most of them leave an owner struggling to sort out whether they've got the right energy, leadership skills, or understanding of their dog's primal nature. At least most agree that dogs are not people in fur coats. Whew, that I get.

It is really quite remarkable that we pay so much attention to wolf behavior when it comes to training our dogs when we haven't been living with and training wolves for thousands of years. It's been dogs who have shared our households, our lives and, for some of us, our livelihoods. You'd think that we'd have enough experience living with dogs to not need to "go offshore" for our training skills and techniques, but we do and the theories abound.

The owner struggling to understand and train their dog has access to a great body of knowledge that can help them make sense of how to change their dog's behavior or get the dog to perform certain behaviors. To me it feels like a golden age of dog training: shock collars are being shelved, the choke chains reserved for a few and you'd be hard pressed to find a trainer today who advocates the use of a rolled-up newspaper for training purposes.

We will probably never stop trying to understand why dogs behave the way they do—and good for us. Let's keep the inquisitiveness alive, anyone working with a fearful dog, or any dog for that matter, should understand that there exists well-documented research and study informing us about the basics of how dogs learn new skills and form the foundation of any modern animal training.

1. Dogs get better at behaviors they repeat. Don't like a behavior? Don't let the dog repeat it.

2. Behaviors that get rewarded will increase. Behaviors that are punished will decrease.

No need for more right now; these two will give you plenty to work with.

A good trainer will help you come up with ways to prevent your dog from practicing behaviors you don't like (from long lines for recalls and crates for housetraining); there isn't the need to worry about who's the pack leader or why Rex chooses your closet as a toilet. Let's just say that dogs don't always come when they are called and have their reasons for pooping in places we find distasteful. A vet visit is one way to find out why your dog is behaving the way it is since some behavior problems may be medical ones.

You don't need a trainer to tell you what is rewarding for your dog, but it is worth noting that what is a reward is determined by the receiver, not the supplier. For some dogs, as with some people, being praised is rewarding (why I might even wash the dishes again it makes my mother so happy), but I'm not likely to go to work 40 hours a week for a pat on the back and a few "you're wonderfuls." But I might enjoy my work so much that I'm willing to do it and not expect to become a millionaire from my efforts; the work is rewarding to me. Chasing a chipmunk (or car) is rewarding to many dogs, no need to toss them a treat for that behavior to get them to repeat it. A door opening can be a reward for sitting quietly in front of it, a ball tossed into a pond can be a reward for bringing it back and a piece of cheese can be a reward for coming when called. (Add to it the opportunity to go back and chase that chipmunk and you've made the recall even more rewarding.)

Images of rulers smacked on wrists and bottoms spanked have set us on a punishment track we find hard to get off of. And, of course, there is the fact that punishment works quite well in changing behavior. Knee your dog in the chest often enough and hard enough and it probably will stop jumping up on you. Holding them up by their leash when they jump up (and threaten their air supply) will likely make them think twice before performing the behavior again, but there are other options for getting the same "no-jumping" behavior that don't end up with a dog going from "happy to see you" to wondering whether something harsh might happen in connection with approaching you.

There is also the risk of fall-out from punishment and too often this is interpreted as further *deviance* on the dog's part.

Punishment does not have to hurt, be loud, or scary to be effective. Move from a sit when the door is opened, the door closes; stay in a sit and the door stays open and the invitation to go out is offered.

When working with fearful dogs it is important that any punishment used does not add to the dog's already formed negative association with the activity or object.

It does not require a treatise on dog behavior or motivation to get your dog to perform the behaviors you're after. A good trainer can offer you ideas and suggestions based on the simple concepts that dogs repeat behaviors they get rewarded for and get better at behaviors they repeat. I'm working on my own theory of why dogs behave the way they do, but I'll save that for another post—I'm still making it up.

"

THE COMBINATION OF GENES AND ENVIRONMENT
AFFECT HOW A DOG BEHAVES. WE DON'T HAVE ANY
CONTROL OVER THEIR GENETIC MAKE-UP, OR EVEN
A WAY TO KNOW WHAT IT IS, SO WE ARE LEFT WITH
MANAGING THEIR ENVIRONMENT IN WAYS TO
REDUCE THE CHANCES THAT A GENETIC
PREDISPOSITION TOWARD FEAR OR ANXIETY WILL
NEED TO BE EXPRESSED.

"

IT'S NOT ALWAYS AS IT SEEMS

Posted February 11, 2009

My own scared dog Sunny was rescued from a 477 dog hoarding site discovered after the hurricanes in 2005. The owner of the site convinced rescue groups that she ran a sanctuary for dogs. She was so convincing that close to 200 dogs were sent to her. Other supposed *rescuers* turned out to work with dog-fighting rings or sold dogs to research labs.

If you decide that you are unable or unwilling to keep a fearful dog, be suspicious of anyone who offers to take her from you. No-kill shelters may be run by hoarders and most cannot offer dogs a decent quality of life. Out of sight may be out of mind but don't be fooled into believing that your dog is going to a better life. No dog lover relishes the thought of euthanizing a dog but, unless you know without a doubt that your dog is going to a place where it will be well cared for and have a good life, keep it in mind as an option.

I know that I would rather have my dog "put to sleep" with a minimum of stress than to have him end up somewhere he will suffer. If you think any life is better than no life I encourage you to visit a few no-kill shelters or sanctuaries where dogs live out their lives on chains, sleeping in dirt, with inadequate food and shelter, no medical care, no play time, no runs in the woods, no ball chasing, no couches to curl up on, no scratches behind the ears, just plenty of fear and misery until they die. Then you can decide whether or not to put that "free to a good home" ad in the local paper.

"

THE IDEA THAT I NEED TO GO AHEAD
OF MY DOGS ALL THE TIME IS SILLY AND
UNREALISTIC. WHAT IF I DON'T WANT
TO GO OUT THE DOOR AT ALL? IF I EAT
BEFORE MY DOGS ARE THEY THEN EXPECTING
ME TO REGURGITATE IT FOR THEM? HOW CAN I
EXPECT MY DOGS TO LOOK TO ME FOR GUIDANCE
AS THEIR LEADER IF WHEN THEY DO COME TO ME
FOR ATTENTION, I IGNORE THEM? THERE IS NO END
TO THE STREAM OF JUSTIFICATIONS PEOPLE COME
UP WITH FOR WHY WE SHOULD PUNISH DOGS.
THERE IS ALSO NO END TO THE STORIES MADE UP
ABOUT WOLF BEHAVIOR TO SUIT THAT PURPOSE.

I AM NOT A DOG. I AM FAIRLY CERTAIN MY DOGS
ARE AWARE OF THAT. MY DOGS ARE NOT WOLVES,
WHETHER THEY KNOW IT OR NOT. DOGS HAVE BEEN
AS SUCCESSFUL AS THEY HAVE BEEN BECAUSE OF
THEIR ABILITY TO FORM TRUSTING RELATIONSHIPS
WITH HUMANS. THIS RELATIONSHIP HAS LED TO
DOGS BEING ABLE TO LEARN SOME AMAZING
SKILLS. WE DO NOT HAVE TO PRETEND TO BE
SOMEONE'S IDEA OF A WOLF MOMMY IN ORDER
FOR THEM TO LEARN THOSE SKILLS.

"

Does My Dog Need Prozac?/Debbie Jacobs

CAN YOU RELATE?

Posted February 28, 2009

I got my first and only puppy when I was sixteen years old. She was a reddish brown fluff ball of eight weeks and I was promptly smitten. My mother did not allow dogs upstairs in our bedrooms so I moved into the basement to sleep with her. When I was not in school (and I admit to skipping classes so I could sneak home and be with her) we were inseparable. I took her with me on the subway into Boston where I let her chase squirrels on the Commons and she would stop in mid chase to return to me when I called her.

I knew nothing about training dogs, at least nothing that was written in books or taught in classes. Treble grew into a handsome dog with feathers on her legs and tail and, when asked what kind of a dog she was, I made up a breed that matched her good looks—a "golden shepherd." She knew to stay with me on walks, sit, lie down, and give her paw on cue—and that's about it. She greeted children with exuberant face licking and she behaved appropriately around chickens and sheep. To this day I can say she was among the most attentive and responsive dogs I've lived with.

Was she an exceptional dog? Certainly to me she was but probably no more so than others. Was I a natural at dog training? Doubtful. What we had was a positive relationship. I did not think of myself as the pack leader, nor did I see any transgressions on her part as challenges to my status as "alpha." We shared the joy of walking on the beach and in the woods. I wanted her to be happy and safe but more than anything I wanted to be with her. Watching her chase a tennis ball made me smile and when I had to put her down because of spleen cancer I was inconsolable.

I learn something from every dog I live with. From Treble I learned that what mattered most was our relationship; and it was not a relationship based on dominance or a social hierarchy, it was a relationship based on what each of us gained by being together. Most of us know this. We greet dogs, offering a treat or a scratch, saying, "Let's be friends." But it's more challenging with a fearful dog and so we too often skip this step, moving onto trying to get behaviors we need to manage the dog.

If you are working with a fearful dog, the first step to take with them is establishing a positive and trusting relationship. Learn what makes the dog feel good; it may be little bits of steak handed out every time you approach, a chest rub, a squeaky toy hidden in your pocket, or a run in the woods. Training and obedience will come in time and will be easier when your dog knows that good things happen when she's with you.

Posted March 10, 2009

Dogs who are afraid of people find very little about being with us pleasant, even if nothing bad is happening to them. Just being near people is enough to get their hearts racing and adrenalin flowing. In order to change how a dog feels about people (or anything it's afraid of, for that matter), you have to provide the dog with some very good reasons. Food is an obvious and powerful reason to think that people may not be all that bad, but for some dogs there may be other, possibly even more valuable, reasons for deciding that sticking around humans is a better response than fleeing.

In my own dog's case I assumed that because he appears to be a border collie mix, he has a border collie's inclination to "do something." Sunny had my other border collie Finn to watch and quickly discovered the joys of running in the woods and chasing after just about anything I was willing to toss. But even if your dog does not have another dog role model, you can make some good guesses as to what activities your dog might enjoy. It's easy to spook a fearful dog so go slowly and, in some cases, ignore your dog while you play with a ball or some other toy until it sparks their interest.

Here are some ideas for playing with your dog:

Name Game: Toss or hand your dog a treat every time you say his name. This not only helps a dog learn his name, it creates a positive association with it.

Treat Toss: Like the Name Game, this simple game consists of tossing treats to your dog. There are some dogs who find the action of catching a treat more rewarding than just being handed one. Try using popcorn for dogs that haven't quite got the catch down.

Hand Shell Game: Hold a treat in one closed fist and offer your dog both hands to sniff or paw at. Open the hand that is "targeted" and show the dog either an empty palm or treat which they get to eat. Start off with a treat in each hand so that the dog can get the idea of the game and win regardless of which hand he chooses.

Outdoor Shell Game: Make piles of snow, leaves, or dirt and hide something your dog is interested in one of the piles. You can start the game by having something hidden in each pile until your dog eagerly goes from pile to pile looking for the hidden treasure. For terriers or other dogs that enjoy digging consider creating an area where the dog can dig. Hide toys or treats in holes for the dog to go after.

Treasure Hunt: Hide treats or toys around the room and let your dog search for them. It's OK for the dog to see you hiding the treasures until they learn the cue to start looking. I say, "treasure hunt!" and they start sniffing.

Any training you do with your dog can feel like a game. My female cocker spaniel is not much for playing but thinks that anything she can figure out to do that gets her a treat is a great game. You can do a search here for books on other games you can play with your dog:

http://www.fearfuldogs.com/books.html

THINKING IS GOOD!

Posted March 26, 2009

S tudies have shown that thinking and learning can slow or even reverse the effects of aging on the human brain. Learning new skills, like playing the piano or line dancing, doing crossword puzzles or brushing up on quadratic equations, is important for humans at any age. It seems that the axiom "use it or lose it" is true for our minds.

I thought about this when I began my journey of working with Sunny. When he first arrived he spent all of his time in a corner of our living room, too afraid to move. After spending all of his life in a pen with other dogs, his brain had not had the chance to develop in the same way my other dogs' brains had. He was also displaying learned helplessness which means that nothing he had tried to do to escape his situation had succeeded so he stopped trying. It was heart-wrenching to see and I wish I had given him a more comfortable place to hide, but I was still acting on training advice that dogs should not be comforted when they are afraid. It is the biggest regret I have in how I have worked with Sunny.

I decided that movement should be a part of his rehabilitation. It began slowly with me enticing Sunny to go after a tennis ball I rolled past him or out into the room. My border collie Finn and old cocker Bugsy helped infuse the activity with excitement, running after the ball themselves. In time we were able to move on to a harness and long line for walks down the dirt road or through the woods.

When I finally let Sunny off the leash to join the other dogs in their explorations of the scents and other delights of the forest, it was a joy to see him behave with enthusiasm and curiosity, exactly as a dog should. His brain was processing new information and hopefully becoming better at doing so. At home I began to work on providing him with novelty in ways which did not frighten him. Many fearful dogs find any changes in their environment scary. I used different bowls to feed him, moved his water dish to accessible but different locations, introduced new toys, and began working on targeting (touching with either his nose or paw) my hand and small objects.

Think about ways you can add new experiences to your dog's life with the goal of arousing their curiosity, not their fear.

Posted March 31, 2009

Too often when we are working toward a goal, whatever it is, we are so focused on the long-term outcome that we fail to notice the progress we're making along the way. This is true when working with a fearful dog as well; we do not notice the small steps our dogs are taking away from fear.

The behavior which makes my heart swell is Sunny's ability to take more and more steps, tentative at first, toward exploration. Even though his body language shouts "wariness," he stretches his neck to sniff a book I've set on the coffee table or takes a few steps into a room he was reluctant to enter in the past. He lingers a little longer in a place he usually races through.

Outside in the woods Sunny is a warrior. He races after the squeaks and chirps of chipmunks and squirrels and he leaps from stone to stone in the river. Inside the house, car, or other building he is a different dog—slinking, resisting, and cowering with an eye always on the exit. I watch the enthusiastic wandering of dogs that aren't fearful as they check out the rooms in my house, racing up stairs and returning with a bone or toy they've claimed as a prize from their discovery mission and I long for the day Sunny will be able to show the same boldness.

Noticing the small steps that Sunny is making is as important as is rewarding him for them. It is not any different from training a dog that is not fearful. All the parts that a behavior can be broken down into need to be noticed and considered. When working on a recall, trainers understand that the behavior is not just the end result of a dog racing toward its owner. It starts with the dog acknowledging the cue, a glance, head turn, spin around, movement toward the owner, and finally getting close enough to be put on a leash if necessary. Each of the pieces of the process should be reinforced.

Find ways to reward your dog for the steps they are making however tiny they may seem. Learn how to use a clicker to make this easier for yourself and clearer for your dog. Keep your goals in mind but don't miss the successes— and be sure to reward your dog for them.

"

THE FIRST TIME WE SEE A DOG PLAY WITH
SOMETHING IS A CAUSE FOR CELEBRATION. NOW
WE HAVE SOMETHING THAT WE CAN USE TO GET A
DOG'S BRAIN-REWARD SYSTEM OILED UP AND CAN
LET FEAR RESPONSES START TO GET RUSTY."

"

HUH?

Posted April 8, 2009

I never gave much thought to the risks of using corrections when training dogs until Sunny, my fearful dog, came into my life. Even the casual "uh uh" that I would use when one of my other dogs' noses was getting precariously close to the cheese on the coffee table would have sent him cowering. I had to find ways not only to get this dog comfortable with me, but I also had to train him. How can you train a dog if you can't correct inappropriate behavior?

When I was growing up, before she headed off to work, my mother would leave pieces of white paper from small notepads (this was pre-Post-its) on the kitchen counter. After school I would return home to find these pieces of paper with benign chores for me to perform written on them. Dust the woodwork, vac the living room, peel potatoes, and the like—nothing horrible except that they were being requested of a kid who would have preferred watching TV, going outside to play, or just doing nothing. I began to dread seeing those notes on the counter. It was years later when I realized how I had been conditioned to feel a certain way about those bits of paper.

My mother sent a care package to me while I was away at college. The box made me feel happy and excited to see what was inside. After slicing through the tape that sealed the box, I lifted the flaps and there on top of my prizes was a slip of white paper on which she'd jotted a note. I felt my stomach tighten and drop. The note was short and positive, "Enjoy! Love, your mother" yet it had elicited in me the same feeling of dread I had experienced for years. I knew it made no sense—the box had good stuff in it—but I could not help my reaction.

So what, you might ask.

We can create similar feelings of dread in our dogs when we pair training with corrections. For some dogs it may not make much difference—they can tolerate a raised voice or collar yank without so much as batting an eye—but for many other dogs their initial reaction to being trained may be an immediate feeling of concern or dread, especially when they do not understand why they are being shouted at or yanked. The timing needed to make punishment effective is not a skill that even many professional trainers have. Unsure of what is expected of them, dogs may delay their response trying to sort out what to do next in order to avoid or prevent the correction. Unfortunately, this can create a cycle of increasingly harsher corrections which, unless the dog catches on quickly, can escalate into a situation which many trainers are familiar with: the owner who professes to have "tried everything" to get their dog to behave the way they want. It's good for business but not so good for the dog whose owner throws up their hands and delivers it to the nearest shelter.

While it is important that owners of fearful dogs pay careful attention to how they work with their pets, it's worth reconsidering the use of corrections when training their dogs. It doesn't mean that you let your dogs go for the cheese on the table; you train your dogs to understand a cue which means stop what you're doing and check in with me for more information.

As for me and those white slips of paper, I got over it; must have been those peanut-butter-filled, glazed, chocolate cake treats that began to accompany the notes.

Posted April 11, 2009

I'm going to keep this one short and sweet. If you are working with a fearful dog you must, at the very least, understand the concepts of counterconditioning and desensitization.

Desensitization is the gradual introduction and increase in exposure to the things your dog is afraid of. The exposure is only increased when the dog exhibits comfort with the situation or object. Go too fast and you set yourself back by causing a fearful reaction to whatever you're trying to get the dog used to. This usually requires more time and patience than people give it. When it doesn't work they blame the concept and not the way they implemented it.

Counterconditioning is the pairing of something the dog is afraid of with something the dog loves. It's classical conditioning except that you're changing a negative association to a positive one. It is often done in combination with desensitization. If the dog cannot engage with whatever you're using to create the positive association (food treats or a toy, for example), then you are not counterconditioning. If your dog will refuse to eat a super favorite treat when someone is 4 feet away, then try having the person be 10 feet away and see what happens. A mistake that people often make is not having the reward be of high enough value, and using enough of it often enough, to outweigh the negative feeling the dog has for the object causing the fear.

A SIGH OF RELIEF

Posted April 25, 2009

This morning while driving home from a yoga class I thought about "relief." While in a particularly challenging pose, trying hard to breathe through it, I could not help but long for the instructor's direction to move from that pose into, "child's pose," a lovely, comfy stretch on the floor. We are repeatedly encouraged not to hurt ourselves but just find our edge and gently explore it. Once out of the pose that had me ready to fall off the edge, I exhaled with relief. Whether it's physical discomfort or emotional suffering, it feels so good to have it end.

Imagine what it would be like to be terrified—truly terrified—on a regular basis and the person that you are suppose to connect with either ignores your fear, whether it's displayed by cowering or snarling, or forces you toward what you perceive to be the jaws of death. Now imagine the relief you would feel if instead that person acknowledged your fear and gently led you away from the horror, reassuring you that all would be well.

There are many ways to help scared dogs, but the first step is to get the dog to trust you. Too many handlers view any refusal or reaction to their demands to be either a challenge to their authority or that their dog is trying to dominate them. A fearful dog is just a fearful dog, doing what it feels it needs to protect itself. So whether it's refusing to follow you down a flight of stairs or growling when you approach its crate, it's just afraid, plain and simple.

I thought about what could be said to someone first embarking on the journey of working with a scared puppy that would be simple to understand. I came up with this: Think about your scared dog as if it were a young child with chubby cheeks and big eyes that gaze up at you adoringly, and then see those eyes go wide with fright and concern. Treat your dog the way you'd treat that young child. Understand that their fear may not seem reasonable to you, but that doesn't change its intensity for them. Consider how you would ease their fears and then take them away and think about how tomorrow you can make it a better experience for them.

We can never know what a dog is thinking but, because we share the same part of the brain that processes fear, it's reasonable to assume that we can imagine what a dog's fear feels like. Hopefully few of us are ever as afraid as many dogs are, but try to imagine what a dog is feeling and then offer them some relief.

CHANGE THE PICTURE

Posted April 28, 2009

It has been years since I have made Sunny hit the dirt and go into panic mode, but that record is over today.

We were all having a nice lie-down; it's close to 90 degrees here. Sunny was with me, calm as could be. I got up and decided to carry an armload of wooden parquet tiles down the stairs. Sunny was next to me. Even though the stack was on a piece of plywood, it was as though the plywood split (it didn't) and the whole stack came crashing down next to and onto Sunny. He fled down the stairs flat as a pancake, crashed into the baby gate at the bottom, and was out the door. Oooops! This would have scared any dog but it has added implications for Sunny since he remains cautious while indoors most of the time.

When I went out to see how he was doing, he was giving me that wide-eyed look that I am so familiar with. I stopped apologizing and said, "Get your frisbee," his favorite game, and up went the tail. He pounced on the frisbee and then tried to get me to take it from him (his second favorite game). Whew.

Finding something that your dog loves and associating it with a verbal cue can come in handy.

"

LEARNING TO PREDICT OR ANTICIPATE
FUTURE EVENTS HELPS AN ORGANISM ADAPT
ITS BEHAVIOR TO IMPENDING DANGERS.

HELPING A DOG LEARN TO PREDICT FUTURE EVENTS
IS AN IMPORTANT PART OF THE PROCESS OF
HELPING THEM COPE. EVEN IF THE FUTURE EVENT
IS SCARY, BEING ABLE TO PREDICT ITS OCCURRENCE
IS BENEFICIAL TO THE DOG.

FIND WAYS TO GIVE YOUR DOG A HEADS-UP WHEN
YOU ARE GOING TO MOVE IN THEIR DIRECTION; GET
UP OUT OF A CHAIR OR BED AND SEND THEM AWAY
BY TOSSING A TREAT BEFORE YOU DO.

"

Posted May 11, 2009

Early during my search for information about how to help my fearful dog Sunny, one rescuer of border collies told me that she 'didn't have the time that I had to work with her dogs'. Her point was that all the desensitization and counterconditioning I was doing might be nice but just making dogs deal with things worked for her, and was faster. I never doubted her success, though I had to wonder if she was working with dogs as shut down and lacking in skills as Sunny.

I have always wondered if I was taking things too slowly with Sunny, but recent conversations with trainers of fearful dogs seem to support my approach. Too often owners and trainers settle for a dog's ability to 'tolerate' its triggers and move on, rather than continuing to work with them until they get to 'completely comfortable' with triggers, or even to 'loving them' if that is ultimately possible.

Imagine if when you asked the owner of a large breed, guard dog, if you could pet their dog, and their response was, "Sure, he tolerates people most of the time," compared to, "Sure, he loves people," would you feel safe with that dog? When someone asked your partner, spouse, or family member how they felt about you and they replied, "Oh I tolerate her," are you as pleased as if they had said, "I enjoy nothing better than being with her."?

When working with a scared or reactive dog the process should be so gradual that the improvements are barely perceptible. This is not to say that one won't ever see leaps in progress with their dog, but most often the kind of changes we want to achieve with our scared dogs occur slowly. It is tempting to get to 'tolerate' and want to plunge on ahead, increasing our dogs' exposure to their triggers.

Only I know Sunny well enough to determine how much he can handle and when tolerating something just isn't enough (vet visits are usually only tolerated by even the most confident dogs). When it comes to his feelings about people

I will not feel safe unless his emotional response to them is joyful and enthusiastic, anything less than that and we run the risk of set-backs or worse, aggression if I increase the pressure on him to be near them. I continue to see improvements in Sunny's behavior around people. Each step forward brings new training challenges, but fortunately both of us do much more than tolerate each other and I hope he's as happy with the company he's sharing on this journey as I am.

Posted May 23, 2009

It would seem that many of us put more thought into what color we're going to paint a wall than we do into thinking about what dog to live with for the next 15 years. I'm not pointing fingers, I am right in there with the best/worst of them. When trainers want a dog to work as a service dog or search and rescue dog or scent detection dog or herding dog or obedience competitor, they carefully consider the temperament and physical capabilities of dogs they adopt or purchase.

Compare that to how many of the rest of us choose a dog:

> "Oh my god she looks just like Muffy, the dog I had as a kid!"

> "Now that is one good looking dog."

> "Awww he's so sad and scared in there."

> "Check out the bold one running around with the toy!"

> "A dog would be good for the kids."

> "I've always wanted a German Shepherd."

Is it any big surprise when we get home and discover that the dog we've chosen may not be the best choice for how we live and what we expect of it? Heck, we even do it with the people we choose to include in our lives, but that's for someone else to blog about.

My parents may have wanted a kid that would be a classical pianist, but they got a kid whose claim to musical fame was that I was able to learn to play *Love Story* really fast. Perhaps, given the right motivation, time, and training, I might have been able to become a concert pianist (we will never know). It turned out that neither my parents nor I really cared all that much about a possible career for me in playing the piano. I'm glad I had the opportunity to learn to play, such as I can, because I think it was good for my brain to practice and learn the skills involved in learning to play, even easy pieces of music fast.

When we find ourselves with a fearful dog it can be disappointing and frustrating. The puppy or dog that was afraid of most everything when its life included only a dozen different things is now afraid of most everything when its life includes hundreds of different things. The dog I'd hoped would join me for swims at the nearby pond can barely tolerate the ride in the car it takes to get there, never mind that the presence of other people is going to dampen his enthusiasm for getting out of the car once we do.

One of the most important and helpful steps I took in regard to my scared dog Sunny was to understand that for whatever reasons he ended up living with me, a good or bad decision on my part, his fears are quite literally, all in his head and it's not his fault. For me to do anything that scares or hurts him is not only counter productive, it's just plain mean.

If you took a baby and kept them tied to a chair until they were two years old, during the time when they learn to walk (and I am not suggesting that you do this, even if you feel like it sometimes), when you untied them not only would they not be able to walk, their brain would be different from the brain of a baby that had been able to move, practice and learned how to walk. A whole bunch of brain circuitry would have been created for 'walking'. A similar sort of thing happens when a dog does not experience variety and novelty during the time when its brain is learning to deal with new stuff, it's brain doesn't have the wiring in place to deal with 'new stuff'. And if that dog was startled and scared on a routine basis, then its brain would develop some very nifty circuitry that caused it to repeat the behaviors it practiced when it was scared. Well... maybe not so nifty.

It happens that brains, both dogs' and humans', are remarkable organs, their ability to change and compensate is astounding. I read a story awhile back about a man who it was found, was missing portions of his brain, a congenital deformity which no one was aware of until he was an adult. He had lived a fairly normal life, different portions of his brain had developed the ability to take over tasks and functions that they might not have otherwise developed the ability to do, had the entire brain been present.

What does this mean for our fearful dogs? To me it means that a dog that was not properly or appropriately socialized needs to change its brain in order to behave and react in ways that we want. The fact that they don't or can't is not their fault, it's just the way their brain works. The process of training or rehabbing them involves encouraging and promoting this change. The same is true for dogs that have learned fearful responses to situations, they too need to change the way their brain responds and reacts. To expect this to happen quickly or easily is to set them up for failure and to set ourselves up for frustration and disappointment. Some changes may never occur, there are no guarantees.

I have come to accept that some of the expectations I have for Sunny might never be realized. I also have seen how given time and training he has made strides and improvements. He has learned skills that make both of our lives easier, less stressful and downright fun at times. It's not his fault that he does not have the brain to deal with certain people or situations, my goal is to help him develop it to whatever extent is possible. In the meantime, he's not playing any concertos, but we do make some beautiful music together.

THE CURIOSITY FACTOR

Posted June 11, 2009

When working with any dog, developing a positive, trusting relationship is important; but when working with a fearful dog, it becomes paramount for the success of training and rehabilitation. There are trainers who have come up with theories as to why dogs behave the way they do and therefore why *their* method of training works best; this includes focusing on things like *prey drive* or being *alpha* to your dog.

There is a large body of research and data which has been collected that informs us as to how animals learn new behaviors. The more fuzzy area of why they behave the way they do leaves a void which too many trainers and owners feel compelled to fill. While most of the theorizing is harmless and may even be correct, some it of it is not and leads to making dogs feel frightened and wary. It is useful to consider that a dog is chewing up the sofa cushions because they are bored or anxious, less useful to believe they are angry or vengeful at being left alone.

Good trainers know that when they have a challenging dog to work with they have to pull out all the stops, strap on their thinking caps, and reach into their bag of tricks. Getting a dog who is afraid of people to buy into what you're selling requires patience and imagination, but there are many routes to take to get their attention. It may be a desire to chase or play that you tap into. Showing your dog that you understand how they feel and will not allow the worst to happen to them, whatever their personal worst may be, is helpful, as is teaching them new more appropriate responses.

One of the fun ways I connect with my fearful dog is to tap into his sense of curiosity. Since novel objects and people frighten him, I need to tread carefully; but in situations in which he feels comfortable he is all dog and wants to check things out. I take advantage of this when working on challenging behaviors like recall. Sometimes my dogs get a treat when they come when called, sometimes a ball toss, or an ear scratch, and sometimes I point out something new and interesting.

If I spy a chipmunk darting into a rotten log I call the dogs, point out the fresh scent and enjoy the show that ensues. Perhaps it's the prints of a deer or moose that I direct them to, or pass around the shards of a newly hatched bird's egg for them to sniff (until one of them gobbles it down). I try to be as predictable as I can be with all my dogs, but especially for my scared dog. I want him to learn that, regardless of how I move or speak, I am never going to do anything bad to him. With a solid history of positive experiences with me, the occasional vet visit or mat brushing does not cause set backs in our relationship. I also look for ways to surprise and delight my dogs, such as leading them to wood piles where they can torment squirrels hidden inside or pulling a new squeaky toy out of a pocket. When I do open my mouth and say their names, I want them to have many reasons for perking up and paying attention and no reason to hesitate.

Posted July 31, 2009

I recently had a brief, somewhat unpleasant email exchange with someone living with a 100-pound American Bulldog that was aggressive to the point of having bitten the owner in the face. From the description of the dog—it had been a timid, cowering in the corner puppy—it sounded as though the dog had learned some effective methods for keeping people and other dogs away from it. The owner was asking about ways to work with a dog that was constantly trying to *dominate* them.

I encourage people to find a local trainer who can help them since it is impossible to accurately assess a dog's behavior and then explain how to work with them via email. It was not my goal or purpose when I created the fearfuldogs.com website, but I understand and empathize with owners who are struggling to find someone they can contact for help. This owner was very clear that they were not willing to pay a trainer to help them with their dog. The potential expenses from vet, doctor, or lawyer bills would far exceed the cost of a trainer, but this argument was not enough to sway them.

The exchange became unpleasant when I tried to explain that their dog probably did not have a dominance problem, it likely had a fear problem. They assured me that they "knew" what dominance looked like: the dog was jumping on them and other dogs and he was growling, snapping, and biting—they weren't stupid! I tried explaining it this way, "If you were afraid of snakes and I came at you with a snake and you pushed me away, were you trying to dominate me?" If you want to use the dictionary definition then sure, the dog is trying to control its environment and if it happens to weigh 100 pounds it stands a good chance of doing that by using the tools at hand, its body and teeth.

The problem is that if you handle a dog with fear issues as though you have a confident dog who is a bully, you are likely to make the fear problem worse. Indeed you might even make the bullying problem worse in a confident dog as well.

If you are five years old and are afraid of someone, you might scream, cry, try to run and hide, or perhaps even struggle (doing little damage if who you're afraid of is bigger than you). But if you're an adult and someone threatens you (i.e., you experience fear because you feel threatened in one way or another), and you happen to have a pistol in your hand, you might pull the trigger. In the future you might decide that brandishing a weapon is more effective than cowering, pleading, or running. As dogs get older and bigger they too can discover that certain behaviors are more effective in making what they want to have happen, happen. So they give up the subtle doggie communications of looking away, yawning, lip licking, rolling over, cowering, or moving away, and replace them with displays of aggression. If subtle displays of aggression don't work (lip raises, growls, or air snaps), they may learn that more intense displays of aggression do, such as, lunging, barking, biting, or muzzle punches.

Trying to stop an aggressive response by using punishment, is not a long-term solution. Yelling at, yanking on, or hitting or kicking a dog that is behaving aggressively can backfire. The dog may redirect its energy toward the handler or someone else nearby. For many dogs the application of any kind of punishment only makes a bad situation worse. They are punished AND the scary thing does not go away. For long-term success in changing a reactive dog's behavior, you must change the dog's emotional response to what scares them AND teach the dog an appropriate behavior which not only works to keep bad things at bay, it provides other rewards as as well.

In a court of law, if a person injures or kills someone who has threatened them, they will likely be treated with leniency. Unfortunately, when a dog threatens or bites someone they will not be shown the same leniency, nor should it necessarily be the case that they are. As much sympathy as I have for a fearful dog that bites, it poses a very real threat. In a court of law and opinion, aggressive dogs usually lose. Fearful dogs who are treated as though they have a dominance problem are likely to become more aggressive, not less. Before your dog needs a lawyer, find a trainer that understands fear-based aggression and how to help dogs that exhibit it.

PRACTICE MAKES....MORE LIKELY!

Posted August 22, 2009

If you are living with a fearful dog who has inappropriate responses to the things he's afraid of (cowering, lunging, barking, growling, fleeing, etc.) it is important to understand something about how animals (including humans) behave when stressed. When your dog is afraid, he is experiencing stress. When an animal is stressed and needs to respond, it is more likely to perform whatever behavior it has performed in the past; you could call this behavior a habit. So your dog may be in the habit of snapping at small children. As long as your dog feels stressed, and this is the habit your dog has, this is the behavior you are most likely to see when small children are near.

People who are required to perform in stressful situations (e.g., police, soldiers, actors, or musicians) will practice whatever behavior is appropriate for situations they may find themselves in. A police officer will practice drawing their weapon, aiming, and firing; soldiers may practice dropping to the ground; actors will rehearse their lines and stage directions; and musicians will practice their piece over and over again. When these people find themselves in a stressful situation they are more likely to be able to perform the behaviors they have practiced, i.e., through training the practiced behaviors have become habits.

In order to help a fearful dog behave appropriately in stressful situations, it's important to give them the opportunity to practice an appropriate alternate behavior at which they can become proficient. This will become the behavior which will replace the one that you don't like. But in order to learn and practice this new behavior, the dog needs to be in a situation in which it does not feel stressed or the level of stress has to be low enough so that they do not revert to whatever behavior has become a habit for them.

The way to learn any behavior is to begin slowly, gradually adding to the difficulty of it. The fewer mistakes made in the process, the less likely those mistakes will be repeated. If you are teaching someone to drive a car, it's best to begin in a parking lot (preferably empty) rather than on a busy highway. If you are working to teach your dog to sit and look at you, it's best to begin in a place where your dog feels comfortable and can focus. As this behavior becomes more reliable in this place you can begin to work in more challenging locations, always striving to practice the appropriate behavior, not the old inappropriate habit.

When it comes to dogs and people, practice may not always make perfect, but it does make it more likely!

I CAN DO THAT!

Posted August 29, 2009

Owners of fearful or shy dogs are often told that they need to build their dog's confidence, but what does that mean? I start with the definition of confidence, which is, to my thinking, the ability to reliably predict that your actions will have a successful outcome. A dog's definition of success will affect whether or not something actually helps them feel more confident.

Some dogs, like some people, seem ready to plunge into life without a thought about potential consequences (e.g., teenage boys), while others seem to hang back and need encouragement and time to try something new. Just watching another dog do something that is scary to a fearful dog is often not enough for a fearful dog to feel confident enough to try it themselves. I could watch people jump out of airplanes all day and I probably would never work up the nerve to do it myself. Anyone that thought that putting me in a plane and tossing me out so I could learn how much fun it was would earn a spot on my s**t list. Yet all too often this is how owners treat their fearful dogs. They may not be tossing them out of planes but they are making them stand still while a small monster pets them, or they put a leash on them and subject them to the attention of gangs of dogs that, for all their dog knows, are out for his lunch money.

Toastmasters International is an organization dedicated to helping people learn the art of public speaking. Regular meetings help people learn how to construct interesting and informational speeches, while giving them the opportunity to stand and practice in front of a supportive group of people. Even with practice and a good speech, finding yourself on a stage with dozens of pairs of eyes staring at you can get your heart pumping and thoughts jumbling out of control. But with the knowledge of how to deal with this physiological effect, it becomes possible to focus on your task and succeed. Each success leads to more confidence in your ability to perform in front of crowd.

To achieve more comfort in this situation you know your speech backward and forward. You practice at home in front of a mirror or with someone you feel comfortable with. You make mistakes and correct them, practicing until those mistakes are fewer and farther between. You learn to take a few deep breaths, slowing yourself down before you jump into action. A good coach will remind you of this as you train. Bit by bit your physical response to being on stage begins to lessen; stage fright may never go away totally but it becomes manageable. And if you make a mistake you discover that it is not fatal, you move on.

For some dogs much of the world is like a stage where their hearts race and their only thought of success is to flee the scene. By working with your dog to teach them skills they can use when faced with what scares them, they can begin to experience success in other ways. They don't need to run away or snarl to keep scary things at bay, turning and walking away works just as well (and gets them a treat and some words of praise for a job well done).

Think about the skills you can teach your dog at home, with praise, encouragement, and good treats before you ask them to climb onto that big scary world stage.

I'VE GOT YOUR BACK!

Posted September 24, 2009

Imagine living with someone who scared you every day, and even if they didn't mean to, they did. Imagine living with someone who at any moment might put you in a situation in which you were scared, and then did nothing! This is how many fearful dogs live their lives—anticipating being scared and then being scared by one thing or another.

The training advice given to people regarding how to interact with their fearful dogs often includes the admonition to "ignore your scared dog," as though paying attention to your dog is going to confirm to them they have reason to be afraid.* Now imagine being with a friend and being afraid of something and, rather than your friend acknowledging that you're afraid, they pretend you don't exist. Does this make you feel better? Now imagine that your friend takes your hand and says, "Don't worry it will be fine." Does this make you more afraid? Hopefully not! Our dogs are not that different from us when it comes to being scared.

I was told a story recently. My husband and I were having lunch with his niece, her husband, and his parents. As is often the case the conversation got around to dogs; I trust you know how that goes! The young fellow's mother shared this story with us about her son:

As a boy he had enrolled in a training class with his beloved dog. It was the first night of class and the trainer had the group walking around the ring practicing heeling. One dog in the class consistently pulled on its leash and the trainer intervened, took the leash from the owner, and "hanged" the dog, lifting it off its feet while the dog flailed and choked. When the procession around the room resumed and the boy and his dog were near the door he turned and walked straight out of the class, never to return. He was not going to let anything like that happen to HIS dog.

I loved the story and I loved the boy (now a man) who knew in his young heart that it was his responsibility to protect his dog. I let my fearful dog know every day that I have his back so he doesn't have to worry and keep glancing over it.

*Ignoring a fearful dog IS often the best way to deal with them when you are new to each other and have not established a relationship with them. By ignoring the dog you are minimizing the risk of being perceived as a threat.

BEHAVIORAL MEDICATIONS
FOR FEARFUL DOGS

Posted December 12, 2009

Behavioral medications can help fearful dogs, so why the reluctance on the part of pet owners to use them? I will share mine.

1. Medications can have side effects that will affect the health of my dog.

2. Medications are a cop-out.

3. I didn't want to medicate my dog.

While there are shy or fearful dogs that can learn new behaviors and change how they feel about things that scare them without the benefit of medications, many more continue to struggle and suffer. This struggling and suffering could be reduced through the professionally supervised use of behavioral medications.

As for my concerns:

1. Yes, medications can have side effects. However, the behavioral medications available for dogs from veterinarians have been researched for their safety and efficacy. Many others, while not specifically labeled for use with dogs, have also provided relief. The list of side effects can be daunting on any medication available today, even routinely used over-the-counter products.

The side effect of fear is stress. Long-term stress has its own long list of health damaging side effects with no benefits. For my dog I decided that the risks of ongoing stress outweighed those of the medications which have helped him. A blood-work panel should be performed before starting any drug regime with a dog.

2. My non-fearful dog with a heart condition was given daily doses of heart medications prescribed by a cardiologist; they did what they were designed

to do and improved her quality of life. I didn't feel as though I was copping out by using them. Another of my non-fearful dogs with low thyroid gets two tablets a day and has since grown a thick coat of fur, stopped suffering from skin infections, and has increased energy. This wasn't a cop-out either. My fearful dog with neurochemical imbalances in his brain deserves the same consideration.

3. The misconception that behavioral medications act as sedatives to calm a dog down is just that, a misconception. Though sedation may be a side effect, it should be short-lived. Do your homework on how behavioral medications can help your dog's brain function improve, making it easier for them to learn new responses to fear provoking stimuli. *From Leashes to Neurons* by Karen Overall DVM is available through Tawser Videos. In it Dr. Overall explains how behavioral medications work and why she views them as powerful tools in the rehabilitation of fearful and aggressive dogs.

There are a variety of non-medicinal approaches we can take to help our fearful dogs, and I recommend that owners learn about these as well. Many can be used in conjunction with prescription medications; check with your vet if you have any questions or concerns.

I have seen the most progress in my fearful dog Sunny through the use of medications. These medications are also the most cost-effective product I have purchased (which may not be a selling point for some folks, but it sure helps when you are caring for multiple dogs). It can take time to discover the medication and dosage that provides the most benefits to your dog. You will need a supportive vet to help you through the process.

Behavioral medications are not cures for fearfulness but, along with a playful training program, they sure aren't cop-outs either.

WHAT ARE WE WINNING ANYWAY?

Posted December 16, 2009

Why are we always keeping score?

I overheard a woman talking about a visit with relatives during which a 5-month-old baby, lying on the floor with a toy, began crying. The woman's son asked her to pick up the baby but she declined claiming, "If I pick him up then he wins." She then went on to prove that she was correct because after being picked up the baby smiled, knowingly as she tells it, as though aware of scoring a point on that round.

As I listened my forehead furrowed and my jaw dropped and it was all I could do to not respond, "What are you talking about!?" Why was she already assuming an adversarial, competitive relationship with a 5-month-old baby? It's a baby, for crying out loud!

I did know what she was talking about though. She was referring to operant conditioning: baby cries, gets picked up, baby learns that crying gets it picked up. Even still I wanted to shout, "SO WHAT!?" What else was he suppose to do, text her? "DIAPER WET PLZ CHANGE," "FOOT STUCK IN JAMMIES HELP." And so what if, heaven forbid, the kid just didn't want to be alone on the floor anymore?

Had she gone on to say that after watching the baby she could see that he was frustrated because a toy had rolled out of his reach and if left alone he could work on solving the problem himself, I might have reacted differently. I admit I am woefully ignorant of how much a 5-month-old is capable of as far as movement and coordination, but at least knowing that she had given thought to why the baby was crying and not that he was just scheming about how to manipulate grown-ups, I would have been less offended by her attitude.

People tend to respond in similar ways to dogs. What part of our fabulous human brains have we shut off when we can look at an 8-week-old puppy, cowering against the back of its cage, the rumblings of a growl in its throat, and think it's trying to dominate us? How someone can watch a dog trembling in fear at the bottom of a flight of stairs and then proceed to drag it up is beyond me. Or have the arrogance of believing we should never allow these displays of emotion. And what emotions are they anyway? It's fear. It's uncertainty. It's pain.

Rather than seeing the baby's smile as an indication that it was aware that he had won a round in a non-existent game, this woman could have smiled herself knowing that the simple act of picking up the baby provided him with comfort and relief. How difficult is it to pick up a baby anyway? How incorrect can it be to teach someone or something that the creatures its life depends on, understands them, respects their points of view, and will care for them?

In this era of creating dominance hierarchies with practically every being we live with, I suspect that we're the big losers.

Posted December 21, 2009

In September 2009 I adopted a 6-year-old female buff cocker named Annie. The previous June my 12-year-old female buff cocker Sabu had died. I was bereft. I knew I could never replace her, but the void left by my cuddly, sweet cocker loomed large for me. With three other dogs in our home it wasn't as though we *needed* another dog, but, like an addict, I was cruising the pages of Petfinder.com looking for my doggie fix. Annie looked enough like Sabu to snag a piece of my broken heart and she was being fostered by a rescue group in Maine—near enough for consideration.

I knew that just looking like my lost girl was not a good enough reason to adopt and wanted to be sure I was also getting a dog that would be comfortable in our home with other dogs. (Living with one *project dog*, my scared boy Sunny, is enough.) I listened for all the euphemisms commonly used to describe dogs with behavioral challenges: not good with kids, would be best as an only dog, takes time to warm up to people, needs a quiet household, prefers to be with people, etc. What I heard was that Annie, though initially reactive to new people and dogs, quickly recovered. I believed (and still do) that the reasons she was being given up had nothing to do with her behavior and decided to bring her home and see how she did.

The description of Annie's behavior was right on. When new people or dogs appear on the scene she begins straining at the leash or rushing toward them, barking and lunging. She eventually settles down, but if another dog responds in kind to having a dog yapping in their face, the potential for a fight escalates. Unlike my other cocker who would give a growl and move away when other dogs were too inquisitive with her, Annie moves in. She did recover from her initial arousal within a few minutes and I decided that it was a behavior I was willing to work with. Compared to Sunny this example of a fear-based behavior seemed minor.

With a behavior display like Annie's it is almost reflexive to raise your voice, shouting to get the dog's attention and pulling back on the leash to keep them away from what has upset them. Unfortunately this is more likely to contribute to the inappropriate behavior than correct it. The first thing I needed to do was to teach Annie to look at me with as little prompting from me as possible. Since she had been loved and well treated, this was easy to do in situations without any distractions. Getting that attention when new people or dogs appear on the scene has taken time and practice, but her volleys of barking and lunging have consistently become shorter.

I have learned to set up situations so that Annie can practice and succeed at being close to a new dog without snapping in their face. With a baby gate separating the dogs, or keeping both on leash out of reach of each other, I reward Annie with high-value food treats for either looking at the other dog or looking at me. She has learned that new dogs on the scene mean something tasty is about to happen. I can see her struggle with her conflicting emotions, that is, a desire to eat treats versus anxiety about the new dog. It is becoming easier to distract her when I see her freeze and stare at an approaching dog, preparing to launch. With time I expect that her anxiety will be overridden by the good feelings she is experiencing because of the treats. She is also practicing a new behavior, looking at me and not barking at the other dog.

Annie has a prejudice against unknown people and dogs. She is no more to blame for her emotional response than I am when I have to pass a group of unknown teenagers hanging out on a corner doing their best to look and act tough. I have the choice to cross the street and avoid the boys or walk past, smile, and say hello. I want Annie to know she has a choice as well—move away from what scares her or greet it politely. From my own experience either of these options leads to a lessening of my own anxiety, and when I do choose to interact with those kids, I find they usually smile and greet me in return.

IT DOESN'T HAVE TO BE TOUGH LOVE

Posted January 18, 2010

Last spring I took care of a friend's dog, a young Rottie named Abby. Abby was living in a family with a senior Rottie and 3 young children. She was a great dog and any challenging behaviors could be chalked up to age and inexperience. While she was with us I treated her as I would my own dogs. We worked on life skills such as not rushing out doors, waiting quietly while I prepared meals, and playing nicely with others. She was a quick study and we all enjoyed having her here.

Not long after Abby's visit my friend commented that it seemed as if they had dropped off a puppy and brought home a dog. I felt a mild blush from what seemed like a compliment until she added, "It's like we sent her to doggy boot camp." The implication made me cringe. Boot camp is rigid, demanding, and often demeaning. I was surprised at her assumption that anything that improved her dog's behavior dramatically must have resembled boot camp. I knew she meant no insult, but I felt a sting.

Abby had played and was rewarded with food treats when she came when called, sat when asked, and responded appropriately with other dogs. I prefer to think that what I offered Abby was a few days at language camp. She learned some common words and had the "culture of human" more clearly explained to her. I was pleased to hear that Abby went home with more of an understanding of how to live with people than she arrived with, but I hope that word of mouth about what I offer dogs does not include the boot camp analogy.

It's not about whipping them into shape, it's about helping them understand and interpret what the people in their lives expect of them. You can love them if you like (or can't help yourself), but there doesn't have to be anything tough about it.

Posted October 11, 2010

One of my favorite podcasts is the *Brain Science Podcast* hosted by Dr. Ginger Campbell, an emergency room doctor in Alabama. Described as the show for "everyone with a brain," Dr. Campbell interviews authors of books on neuroscience. Of special interest to me was her interview of Jaak Panksepp on affective neuroscience.

The latest *Brain Science Podcast* (BSP 70) is an interview with Dr. Scott Lilienfeld, co-author of *50 Great Myths of Popular Psychology: Shattering Widespread Misconceptions about Human Behavior*. The conversation focused on the fact that scientific reasoning and critical thinking do NOT come naturally. Instead, we all tend to make similar errors, such as mistaking correlation for causation.

Those of us working with dogs would do well to make note of this tendency since it happens all the time when we are trying to change behaviors in dogs, as well as trying to figure out why something is successful or not. I am reminded of a comment made by a trainer who said, "We have all the theories, dogs have all the facts."

Dogs often learn *despite* what we do, not *because* of what we do. For example, the unfortunate practice of *dominating* a dog with the use of physical force is often heralded for producing miraculous changes in a dog's behavior because of its relation to how wolves and dogs communicate within their own social groups. Yet when we look at the research that has been done, we find that the norm for dogs and wolves is NOT a social hierarchy maintained only through the use of force or aggression. This is not to say that they don't behave aggressively or that fights over resources do not occur, but that social order is, for the most part, maintained through social conduct which is cooperative more often than competitive, even when there is a top-ranking animal.

When we assume that a dog changes their behavior to suit our preference because in the course of dominating them we have gained their respect because they now know we are the leader of the pack, we need to consider that what we might have accomplished instead was to have caused the dog to fear us. While fear of retribution or punishment is a popular way of maintaining social order—governments and gangs use it quite effectively—is it really the relationship we want to have with our dogs? Dr. Robert Sapolsky documents how living with constant stress contributes to illness, and that stress can be psychological as well as physical. The threat of punishment, especially if it is used routinely to manage or control behavior, can add to the stress a dog is already experiencing.

We'd expect a chuckle if we were to claim that our dog's ability to perform well on an agility course was due to the lucky red undies we were wearing. Yet again and again we hear theories on why dogs perform behaviors, theories which have no basis in fact. While there are vast areas of animal behavior that we do not have science-based research on, there are many areas in which we do.

Interacting with our dogs in ways we perceive to be the same as the ways they communicate with each other, may not work for the reasons we think they do. Wearing our lucky red undies when training may be a safer bet.

NO, YOU GET OVER IT!

Posted February 12, 2010

When people talk about their fearful dogs I often hear the question, "How do I get him past (or over) his fears?" It's as though fear is a location that a dog just needs to journey through. Although it makes a nice metaphor—the image of a path from a place of anxiety to one of confidence—I think it also leads people to envision forward movement. And if a dog is unwilling or incapable of making that movement on his own, all we need to do as his owners is make him move. Afraid of a flight of stairs, walking on a new surface, getting into the car, or little kids, here, let me help you by dragging you by the neck. Unfortunately for dogs, this can work for some, leaving trainers and owners to believe that it's the route to take for getting a dog past his fear. Movement can help dogs in many ways but it doesn't have to be forced marches.

I consider myself fortunate that I have not had a life filled with constant fear and dread. I find it hard to imagine what that must be like. Perhaps an inadequate substitute that I can imagine is being cold, the kind of cold that keeps your muscles tensed and your breath short and rapid. I don't think I will ever get over or past being cold. When I'm cold like that, as it seems I have been a lot this winter, what I notice the most is the comfort of warmth. My shoulders relax, my chest loosens, and I sigh audibly. It feels so good not to be cold.

Rather than trying to think of ways to get my dog over his fear, I begin by thinking of how I can help him find relief from his fear. Often it's management and the control of his triggers or his proximity to them, but it also includes giving him the training and skills to make safe and appropriate choices when he's around a trigger. Sunny can find relief in moving away from people who scare him or by sitting and waiting for me to decide what our next move will be. After four years together I think that Sunny is able to predict that my next move is going to be one that provides him with relief, and doesn't force him to get past or over anything.

"

MEDICATIONS. THEY DON'T CURE FEARFULNESS
BUT THEY CAN HELP A DOG PERFORM NEW
BEHAVIORS THAT WE CAN MAKE SO REWARDING
THEY'LL WANT TO PERFORM THEM AGAIN!

"

Does My Dog Need Prozac?/Debbie Jacobs

DROP THESE D'S

Posted February 20, 2010

I am constantly trying to eliminate the belief and the feelings I get when I assume that dogs' failures to respond to my requests are due to their choosing to be disobedient, defiant, or dominant. Not that dogs don't necessarily have these as motivations for behaving inappropriately, but most dogs, and especially fearful dogs, likely have other things going on.

Staying with me for the next ten days is lovely little Stella, who looks like a corgi/beagle mix. When I first met Stella she was unable to approach me and needed to drag a leash so I could get her to go in and out of the house as needed. Her owners have done great work with her and, although her first reaction to new people is to be startled, she recovers quickly and has become one of those lucky fearful dogs that once they get to know you is playful and happy.

Today as we headed out for our daily woods walk all the dogs eagerly scampered out of the house except for Stella. Stella lagged behind, looking out of the open door but not moving through it. I admit that my initial response to this behavior was a tinge of impatience and frustration, "Geesh, come on already." I had to remind myself that Stella was probably uncomfortable either going through the door and/or going past me, not uncommon problems for fearful dogs.

As with any behavior we are after with our dogs, there are different ways to get them. We can be sure that the dog knows how to perform the behavior and understands our cue for it. I could have put a leash on Stella and had her walk in and out of the door with big rewards as we did so. I could teach Stella to target my hand, or something in my hand, and use that behavior to help her move through doorways.

Since Stella has gone in and out of doorways before without hesitation, I decided that there was something about the way I was asking for the behavior that caused her reluctance to follow the other dogs. Even if her owners used a different cue, it doesn't take much thought for a dog to follow a gang of excited dogs out the door. She wasn't afraid of the other dogs so I assumed I was the problem. I changed how I was standing at the door, turning my body slightly and avoiding direct eye contact as I invited her out. I waited a few seconds and when she didn't comply I shut the door and moved away for another few seconds. I tried it again and on the third offer she came right out the door when asked.

It's easy to become frustrated and impatient with a dog, especially if we think that they are behaving in ways that are meant to defy or confront us. Keep in the front of your mind that it's often not a dog's unwillingness to comply, but their inability to do so that prevents them from doing what is being asked of them.

EVOLUTION ANYONE?

Posted February 21, 2010

I watched a 28-second video yesterday of a trainer in Canada doing some pretty rough stuff to a dog. The abuse that he inflicted on the dog included sharp collar jerks, pulling the dog off its front feet, and slapping the dog on the face. It was unclear what the dog (a large breed, perhaps a vizla or Rhodesian) had done or was doing to provoke this kind of treatment. The setting appeared to be an outdoor training class with other people and their dogs circled around. The dog being abused was barely moving, which may have been the *problem* in the trainer's eyes; I don't know. The creator of the film claims that the trainer was annoyed with the dog's owner and took his ire out on the dog.

When I watched the clip I got that heart-constricting feeling that occurs when my body has a reaction to seeing not only someone/thing suffering, but also a response to the perpetrator of the violence. I prefer not to fantasize about being violent toward other people, but in this case I had flashes of what I would do had I been there to witness it. It was shocking to watch a group of pet owners, who no doubt care about their animals or else they wouldn't be bothering with a training class, standing around while someone assaulted an animal. Whether anyone spoke up for the dog I couldn't tell. It may have happened so quickly that there was little chance to react and, while some may have been dumbstruck by the treatment, others may have assumed that it was justified.

In the clip I saw the film had been looped so that it looked like the dog was being yanked and hit several times. This was unfortunate since it was not explained that this editing had been done. More unfortunate is the idea that yanking and hitting a dog once isn't that bad, and only if it happens repeatedly that there is a problem.

Some may criticize me for using terms that are usually applied to violence against people to an animal, but what else is it other than assault when someone has another being trapped by a chain around their neck and proceeds to hit and choke them? Oh wait, there is another name for it, it's called TRAINING by folks like this guy!

Why is it that we are drawn to watching people who gain control of other creatures through the use of intimidation and physical violence? Is it because we don't define what we are seeing as violence? Is getting what we want when we want it, exactly as we want it, enough to justify the means we use to get it? Who finds these people and then popularizes them by giving them TV programs and guest appearances on talk shows, and why do they do it other than to make a buck (or millions of them)? We are sickened when we watch programs that advocate the teaching of violence to young children (Yes, Virginia, there are people who do this.), yet tune in weekly to learn how to bully, threaten, scare, and hurt dogs without the bat of an eye. It surprises me how many otherwise intelligent, thoughtful people do not see violence against animals for what it is, violence, period.

I have four dogs and board others at my home. I understand what it's like to feel frustrated and angered by their behavior. It seems that in the spectrum of human behavioral responses to being frustrated and angry, violence comes more easily than thoughtfulness and patience. There is probably an evolutionary reason for this, but it seems a poor excuse when we are capable of measured, productive, non-violent responses. As a species we find reasons to justify our bad behavior whether we are enslaving other people, beating them up for being different than us, or eating a piece of cheesecake and, although they are not comparable, they are evidence that we can delude ourselves about minor and major things.

Many who are moving up the evolutionary ladder are happy to give a hand to those lingering a few rungs below.

THEIR BRAINS MAKE THEM DO IT

Posted February 23, 2010

I recently heard about a study that was done using functional Magnetic Resonance Imaging (fMRI), a type of specialized MRI scan that measures the change in blood flow related to neural activity in the brain of humans. This technology makes it possible to see which neurons are active in a brain when certain thoughts or emotions occur. The study looked at neurons in the brain's amygdala, which is responsible for emotional reactions, and the visual cortex, which *sees* objects. What they found was that when presented with photographs of images intended to induce positive or negative emotional responses, regardless of the content, it was the neurons in the amygdala which reacted first. What this indicates is that even before we *know* what we are looking at, we have already have had an emotional response and its accompanying reaction caused by the autonomic nervous system.

Since dogs and other animals share these same parts of the brain with us, it's likely that their brains respond in a similar way to stimuli—and it makes sense. A gazelle grazing on the plains is probably not going to live to graze another day if it stops to think about whether or not an animal moving rapidly toward them is a lion. In much the same way, most of us will leap back if we step off a curb when we notice that a car is speeding toward us; we do it without any conscious thought as to how fast the car is traveling or whether it is likely to make contact with us based on its speed. We can thank our amygdalas for this.

Think about how this affects our fearful dogs and the way they are often handled. By the time a dog appears to see whatever scares it, its brain has already had the opportunity to respond negatively to it. In many cases the negative emotional response is accompanied by a negative behavioral response like aggression. We know that dogs get better at any behavior they have the opportunity to repeat, whether we approve of it or not. So each time we put our fearful dogs into situations in which they are exposed to whatever scares them enough to cause a response, they're getting better at that response.

Trainers who use force or intimidation to stop or control inappropriate responses in these situations are, in effect, closing the barn door after the horses are out. It's not the behavior they need to stop, it's the emotional response. Hurting, scaring, or threatening a dog to stop it from feeling frightened makes no sense. When the focus is on the aggressive display (or the animal's reluctance to perform a particular behavior), they've missed the proverbial boat. This is why desensitization and counterconditioning do help fearful dogs; they change the emotional response a dog has to whatever scares it. The brain is changed so that the first reaction it has is a positive rather than a negative one.

Any of us who have tried or are trying to do this know how slow and tedious the process can be. But the next time you see a trainer responding to a dog's fear-based behavior with the use of force or punishment, I hope your own emotional response is a negative one.

Posted March 30, 2010

A light-bulb moment occurred for me in regard to my fearful dog Sunny when I understood that he was limited in his abilities by his brain. It wasn't that he was consciously choosing not to come to me or refusing to move out of the corner; it was that, given the development of his brain, these behaviors were how he was *wired*, so to speak, to perform. Any changes I wanted to see in him were going to have to be connected to changes in how his brain worked.

Although Sunny will likely always be limited in some ways by the deprivation of his early life or possibly a genetic predisposition to startling easily Sunny has been able to find ways to achieve certain goals despite his disadvantages; his brain has changed. Not too long ago it was thought that the brain that you were born with was the brain you had for the rest of your life; you could take advantage of what you had, or not. Now it is understood that brains are far more plastic than anyone ever realized. You can make a brain work better through stimulation, stimulation that does not cause chronic stress.

What is stimulating to a brain? Just about everything! Sounds, smells, physical sensation, movement, problem solving, and novelty. A major problem for many dogs is that they did not experience novelty during their early brain development. Being stuck in a cage at a puppy mill, tied to a tree in a backyard, or stuck in a hoarder's home limit the novel experiences a dog has. Even well-loved and cared for dogs can suffer when they are not exposed to other dogs, noisy children, cars, etc., in safe ways when they are young. The lack of exposure to novelty makes it scary when something new appears on the scene, or the dog is put into a new environment. The pattern can then be set, i.e., new things are scary, even if they cause the dog no harm.

Because brains can change, and introducing novelty is a way to do it, people living with fearful dogs can look for non-threatening ways to change what their dog experiences. Moving food and water bowls to different locations, leaving different toys out for the dog to investigate, playing calming music, massage, moving furniture for the dog to navigate around, or introducing new scents to the environment are just a few of the ways you can add novelty to a dog's world. Sunny takes agility classes for the non-habitual movement the courses require him to perform. We practice obedience skills and learn new tricks to encourage him to think and figure out what is expected of him.

Living with an extremely fearful dog added stress to my life, but the novelty sure has been worth it!

REWARDING REACTIVITY

Posted April 29, 2010

It's interesting to look back at my life and see where the paths of knowledge or interests I've followed began. In high school, back in the 1970s, I was having a tough time getting myself to classes. A creative guidance counselor arranged for me to volunteer, in lieu of attending classes I did not need to graduate, at a variety of organizations in the Boston area—one was a day-care center for autistic adolescents. It was here, with a pocketful of M&Ms, that I was first introduced to behavior modification and positive reinforcement. I was assigned the task of teaching one of the boys to hang up his shirts. This was my first experience using *back chaining* to teach a behavior. The first skill he was taught was to put his shirt, already on a hanger, onto the closet rod, then we worked back from there.

One of the greatest delights in my life was a cocker spaniel named Sabu. Sabu and her mother, Mitzi, came to live with us after their owner died. Both dogs were among the cutest and sweetest cockers on the planet, as I came to learn when different vets or trainers we encountered over the years commented on their temperaments. My friend John bred a litter or two a year and the pups had an idyllic life on 180 acres in rural New Hampshire. As soon as the pups were old enough, he packed them up in a picnic basket and brought them along when he traveled. They went for car rides, attended contra dances, and were fussed over by children and adults, as is the lot of these cuter than stuffed animal dogs. I joked that neither Sabu or her mother ever met a person they didn't think could open a refrigerator door. They greeted new people like long-lost friends, a behavior I encouraged when they first arrived to live with me. Children got a handful of treats to reward the girls for performing a simple trick. At the time terms like "positive reinforcement" or "classical conditioning" were not yet part of my vocabulary.

While Mitzi was a confident flirt around both people and other dogs, Sabu was timid with dogs and, although never aggressive, displayed obvious discomfort when she was approached by them. Once all the sniffing was over she was fine, but when a nose was aimed for her butt she plunked it down and cast warning glances at any dog that was intent on invading her personal space. Unfortunately, over the years when I fostered dogs for our local shelter, there were occasions when an exuberant and often clueless larger dog bumped into her or knocked her over. She began to visibly cringe when dogs ran past her until ultimately one day she stopped joining me for our daily woods walks.

I felt terrible about this and came up with a plan for getting her to rejoin me. It started with a pocketful of treats. After coaxing her to join me on a walk, whenever a dog raced past her, I called her to me and gave her a treat. Soon a dog passing her was the cue to turn around and come to me for a treat. As time went on her cringing diminished and I had to change the rules; a dog had to run by her and either graze her or come within a few inches in order for her to get a treat. She had begun taking the opportunity to notice dogs moving past her, whether they were 1 foot or 10 feet away, and then she would spin around to get her treat. The experience of being out with other dogs was no longer fraught with worry but had become a nonstop opportunity to get treats. The emotional landscape of the experience had changed for her and the challenge of cutting back on the treats was less of a concern to me than the fact that she was back enjoying our walks together.

It was years later when I was boarding a reactive cockapoo that I pulled this technique out of my back pocket. This little brown cockapoo was OK with other dogs most of the time, but she responded aggressively to dogs running or moving closely past her. With this girl I started by creating a strong history with the conditioned reinforcer, "Yes!" She was a quick study and when we were out for our walks I decided that of all the behaviors she performed in relation to other dogs—looking at them, running toward them, sniffing them, or barking at them—were acceptable. The only behaviors that were completely unacceptable to me included making contact with another dog's head, with either her feet or mouth or using her teeth on any part of their body.

With this dog instead of calling her to me as I did with Sabu, I began to mark with "YES!" any of the behaviors which were acceptable, even if they led up to the inappropriate behavior. I tried to catch the behavior chain early on if I could, marking the moment when her eyes locked on her target; but even if I wasn't successful and she began to head for the other dog before I could call out "YES!" she'd still stop the chase and return to me for a reward. Early on in this process I was marking her behavior frequently, paying close attention to any interest she showed in another dog. One day I watched as she raced toward another dog and, before I could get the word out of my mouth, she stopped next to the dog and turned to look at me as if to say, "Is this what you want me to do?" This was a pivotal moment because I was not managing her behavior, she was! Once this happened it became easier for me to shape the behavior so that the arousing chases became shorter and shorter.

Little did I know back in high school that one day I'd be substituting liver treats for M&Ms, or that modifying behaviors could be so exciting.

"

DOGS MAY HELP US MORE THAN WE KNOW.
BY BEING CATALYSTS FOR US TO LEARN ABOUT
FORCE AND COERCION-FREE TRAINING METHODS,
THEY MAY BE ENCOURAGING US TO EVOLVE.
SURE OUR INNER CHILD LOVES HAVING A DOG
AROUND, BUT WHEN WE ARE FACED WITH HAVING
TO DEAL WITH THE BEHAVIOR CHALLENGES
OF A SCARED DOG, IT'S OUR INNER ADULT
THAT WE NEED TO TAP INTO AND LEARN
AND GROW AS A COMPASSIONATE HUMAN
AND SKILLED TEACHER.

"

Does My Dog Need Prozac?/Debbie Jacobs

DON'T TAKE MY LEAD ON THIS ONE!

Posted May 14, 2010

Sunny came to us with no skills for interacting comfortably with people. That was obvious, but what wasn't obvious to me at the time was that being in a house was also a horrifying experience for him as well. It was winter in Vermont when he first arrived and, having grown up in an Arkansas hoarder's compound, being an outdoor dog was not an option for him here where temperatures dip below freezing. Rather than provide Sunny with a cozy, secure place to hide, I set him up in a corner of our living room. I thought, incorrectly, that giving him a crate to retreat to would only be enabling his fears. Ugh. To date it's one of the biggest regrets I have about how I handled him. Chalk it up to ignorance and naiveté.

My first attempt to take him for a walk on leash almost ended in disaster. Like a kite plummeting to earth in a windstorm, Sunny bucked, pulled, spun, and leaped, nearly slipping his collar. Without his collar there is little question in my mind that I would never see him again. I've seen other dogs "kiting" at the end of leashes and it sends waves of horror and pity through my body. The fear and desperation the dog is experiencing is palpable. So for weeks Sunny lived huddled in his corner surrounded by papers. Other than shifting his position from one direction to another, he didn't leave this spot, even if he was alone in the house. To discover whether he was having exploratory forays on his own, I would leave tidbits of food on the floor around the room returning to discover them where I'd left them. I doubted he had even checked them out and left them untouched.

When I decided it was time to take Sunny outside for walks I fitted him with a harness that he could not slip out of, encouraged him out of the house, and promptly almost got dragged off my feet as he tried to flee from me. Getting him back into the house was the opposite experience. Luckily for me, though sad for him, Sunny seemed to discover that his only option was to give up and go wherever the current dictated, so I never had to pull him, feet dragging, to get where we needed to go. On the occasions when it was apparent he could not move I would pick him up and carry him; the alternative of yanking him along was too distasteful to me.

In order to defecate while on a leash Sunny had to get as far from me as he could, circle and then squat, his eyes wide and locked on me. Because I rarely walk my dogs on leash, my collection was limited to 4-5' lengths or the short slip leashes embossed with names of vet clinics on them. I had seen retractable leashes (the kind with a large plastic handle into which a cord or flat nylon line pulls out and coils back automatically) and purchased the longest I could find. After I had, without too much damage to my person, figured out NEVER grab the line to stop the dog at the risk of slicing my fingers off, and had sorted out the button for keeping the line from either extending or retracting, it seemed to fit the bill. Sunny could move away from me, and with only one hand I could manage the leash.

Early one winter morning I attached the leash to Sunny's harness and, as I cracked open the storm door, he bolted out; when all 50 pounds of him hit the end of the leash, I was pulled face first into the door. The crashing and sound of my surprised (and unprintable) shout frightened Sunny again and, thwarted in his attempt to escape into the trees, he headed down the driveway. I had managed to step outside the door and as Sunny advanced back toward the house the leash retracted and as he continued past, extended until he hit the limit and I was pulled around and this time stopped when I was slammed into the side of the house.

In retrospect I wish one thought had crossed my mind, "Cut your losses," and had reeled him in and called it quits for the day; but he was due for a walk. As events unfolded I had the distinct impression that it looked like a scene of choreographed slapstick and might have been comical if Sunny wasn't so terrified and I hadn't ended up with a bleeding gash on my forehead.

It was only during our walks down the dirt road alongside the river that I ever got glimpses of what normal might look like for Sunny. His movements would loosen up, he'd sniff and explore, urinating on special spots which only made sense to a dog. He needed this walk. Bundled up in my powder blue down jacket which I had bought years before for winter camping and which was rated to -40°, I looked like a toddling Michelin man, a hat pulled down to meet my glasses which now sat cockeyed on my face, bent from my run in with the house. Smudges of blood remained on my cheeks as I'd wiped it out of my eyes.

Sunny loosened up after about a mile of walking and as we were headed back a neighbor pulled up next to us in his car. It was a weekend morning and I'd hoped that we'd make it through the walk without any passing cars, but, as folks are apt to do in rural areas, he slowed down and stopped for quick chat. When he opened his window and looked at my face his eyebrows flew up and he asked, "Are you OK?" The walk had helped both Sunny and I calm down, but my chest was still constricted and felt like every fiber was pulled taut. The fear, pain, and frustration I had felt from simply trying to exit the house with Sunny had not dissipated completely. I held back tears and tilted my head slightly toward Sunny who had run to the end of the leash up into the trees lining the road, "Yes," I responded and he gave me a grimacing smile laced with pity, understood I was not in the mood for a conversation, and drove off.

On my return home, my husband who had not seen our dramatic departure came outside to greet us. The emotional edge that I had been teetering on slipped out from under me when he said, "Oh, My God! What happened?" Tears started flowing and I sobbed, "This f**cking dog!" When John reached to take Sunny from me I knew it wasn't a good idea, but I wanted someone to step in and make it better or make it all go away. As he took the handle of the retractable leash and grabbed a hold of Sunny's harness and pulled him in the house I blurted out, "Don't scare him!" But Sunny, who had been perched on an emotional edge over a much deeper and darker abyss than I can ever imagine, was about to go tumbling down.

After putting Sunny into the house, John stepped back outside and the noises we heard next coming from inside horrified us. I have never heard a dog being killed but the shrieking we heard was what I imagined it would sound like. There were crashes and thuds and I thought the other dogs must be attacking him—a possibility that was not only unlikely, it was impossible since all the other dogs were outside with us. Back inside I surveyed the scene and deduced what most likely had happened.

After getting Sunny into the house John, unversed in the finer points of retractable leashes, had let go of both the harness and the extended leash which dropped to the floor and then zipped toward Sunny, hitting him and sending him into a blind panic. He rammed into the sliding-glass door, lost control of his bowels—spraying the wall, doors, and couch—knocked over a large potted plant, and raced to his latest safe spot under my desk in our office which is where I found him, panting, exhausted, eyes glazed over. He appeared physically uninjured but to this day I cannot say whether or not that experience left him with other scars.

As I cleaned the walls and glass doors the realization that all the well-meaning advice I'd been given about how to handle a fearful dog was just not cutting it for me or Sunny. He needed more than time and love. He wasn't snapping out of it, nor was forcing him to do things that scared him helping either. I needed better information and more help, but first I needed a new damn leash!

JUST WHAT IS IT WE EXPECT?

Posted June 15, 2010

My border collie Finn has a high tolerance for pain. When his attempt to herd an SUV a couple of summers back proved to be a dismal failure, I was amazed, and at the same time heartened, to see his tail wag as I carried him into the vet's office—a hind flank degloved, opposite hind-leg broken, fractured pelvis, and other lacerations—when the staff greeted him. Shock was likely providing him some degree of numbing, but it still couldn't have felt good. Keeping him from overdoing it on any limb that has shown tenderness is a challenge when the opportunity to run after something presents itself, unlike my cocker who when sore or injured would scream in anticipation of the pain.

So I was surprised when Finn snapped at the vet's hand when he was having stitches removed from a paw pad. I was equally surprised by the vet's response; she shouted at him and popped him on the nose with her fist. It wasn't her physical response that surprised me—it must be tough working with clients who can send you in for stitches yourself—but rather it was her emotional response that surprised and disappointed me; she was angry with him.

More than the reprimand and the pop on the snout, it was her lack of acknowledgment that he had a good reason for his behavior that didn't sit right with me. I'm not making excuses for my dog's behavior, I don't need to, he didn't do anything wrong, though he did do something we didn't like. He applied a controlled bite to try to stop something that was painful to him. After suffering through several stitches he couldn't tolerate it anymore. He needed a break and this was his way to get that point across.

I communicated recently with a woman who was having trouble with her dog on walks; he would stall in certain places. A physical exam showed no apparent reason for the dog's reluctance and hesitation to go for walks, and the fact that he was a fearful dog led us to assume that something was scaring him. The concepts of desensitization and counterconditioning were explained but the owner was concerned that her dog might just be being "stubborn." What did she mean by that?

When people use the word stubborn to describe their dog (or any other animal for that matter), they typically mean that they can't get the dog to do what they want it to do. Just because she couldn't figure out why the dog was behaving the way it was didn't mean the dog didn't have a reason for choosing one behavior over another. We don't have to like what a dog is doing (or not doing), but we sure as heck need to accept that it's important enough to the dog to affect his behavior.

Why is it that we expect things from our dogs that we don't even expect from ourselves or other people? When working with fearful dogs, it can help if we change our thinking by changing a few words in our assessment of their behavior. It may not be that they *won't*; it may be that they *can't*. Instead of being upset and punishing the *won't*, help them learn new skills so that they *can*.

DUKE

Posted July 4, 2010

While staying with friends in Costa Rica, I had the chance to watch a family interacting with their 7-month-old terrier-mix pup. Duke (unfortunately pronounced "Dookie" in Spanish) was everything you'd want in a dog—engaging, playful, responsive, friendly, and cute to beat the band. He was a classic little scruffy Disney character.

My Spanish is limited so when the father of the family began to order Duke around (to show me his trick of rolling over), I realized that both Duke and I were in the same boat—neither of us understood what he was saying. I watched Duke as he tried his best, dropping to his belly, rolling onto his back, but even as the commanding voice got louder and the hand gestures accompanying it grew bigger and more expansive, Duke stayed belly up, unsure what his next move should be. Finally when the rollover never occurred, Dad waved it off with a laugh and made a disparaging remark about the dog's intelligence.

This experience highlighted for me the challenges dogs face in trying to learn what the heck we want from them. I suspect in Duke's case he figured out what made the loud, commanding voices stop and did that. Perhaps he had done complete rollovers for his owner, but with the pressure on both dog and owner to perform, staying in a classic "Please don't hurt me" position seemed the safest choice for little Duke, especially since he was rewarded for the behavior with the cessation of shouting in the past.

The translation challenge extended to my own interpretation of Duke's behavior. I cut up cheese into small pieces and began to teach Duke to spin. In between spins Duke sunk into a down position. I thought that perhaps this was a behavior he had been reinforced for in the past and he used it as a default. I began to reinforce a stand position, but inevitably Duke slipped into a down position. I joked to his owner that he was a lazy boy and we shared a laugh about that until it occurred to me that indeed Duke was actually slipping down. The floors in the house, typical to many homes in Costa Rica, were ceramic tiles. They were so clean and shiny that on several occasions I did a double take thinking they were wet.

When I got Duke spinning again I kept an eye on his feet and could see that when he wasn't lying down, his furry paws would slide on the floor. Whether standing or sitting, he constantly had to adjust his footing to keep his feet under him. When he was sitting, his front paws gradually slid forward and, rather than fight gravity, he simply went with it and ended up lying down.

How often do we get frustrated with our dogs for not doing what we ask? They may have no idea of what we want or when physical constraints prevent them from doing it. I'll guess that this is more common than dogs deliberately not doing what we ask when they understand and are fully capable of performing a behavior and choose to blow us off. Duke was lucky; the only punishment he received for noncompliance was some good-natured name-calling. Those were words I did understand in Spanish!

BOND!

Posted July 19, 2010

On Monday nights at 9:15, a fabulous group of dog lovers moderate an exchange of ideas on twitter using *Tweetchat*. Called "#dogtalk," the topics vary as professionals, specialists, and enthusiasts are invited to be guest tweeters.

The conversation drifted to fostering a dog as people shared their experiences of caring for dogs that were destined to leave them for homes of their own. Finding good foster homes is a challenge for many rescue groups; it can mean the difference between life or death for many dogs. Many of us admitted to failing at fostering; the dog that was suppose to be with us for only a short time was still snoozing on the couch years later. It's not always easy to give up these dogs.

Some foster caregivers might worry about a dog forming too strong an attachment to them. Emotional attachments are responses to a person, place, thing, or experience and usually are the result of positive associations (though not always, but I'm not a psychologist so won't comment on this phenomenon). I remember how difficult it was to get rid of my old VW Rabbit which I had driven cross-country 3 times during my years at college in California. It was just a car—one with a rusted out fuel tank at that—yet I hated to see it go. I loved that car and suspect I'd love it even more today with its diesel engine and almost 40 miles to the gallon fuel efficiency. A new pickup truck helped get me over that loss.

I think of bonding as a skill, and being given the opportunity to develop that skill is important. Attachment and bonding are about building relationships and having the neurochemistry in place to assure that it can happen. There are ways in which brains can go awry when it comes to forming attachments with things as in the case of hoarders or, perhaps, when people love their cars too much. The consequences to humans who spend their infancy and early childhood without the benefit of developing bonds with caregivers can be tragic.

There are fearful dogs who are able to form attachments to their primary caregivers but not easily with other people. The first time I met my (not fearful) border collie Finn, I paid attention to how he responded to the people and dogs around him. He was friendly and outgoing with the strangers, polite and appropriate with the dogs, but what clinched the deal for me was how he behaved with the woman who had been taking care of him. He was showering her with attention and face licks. I knew that if he was able to bond with her he'd bond with me. We are by my count his seventh home, including the three shelters he'd ended up in and, unless he was born at the first, he'd lived with at least three other people or families. However disruptive that might have been for him, somewhere along the way he'd learn to form attachments with humans. When he came to live with us he was an old hand at it and I'm grateful to the people who handled him so compassionately.

So while you might want to guard your own heart when it comes to fostering a dog, help them develop the ability to connect and trust humans; it's a skill that will serve them well when they find their forever home.

CRIMES OF PASSION

Posted August 12, 2010

As humans, despite the incredible ability to think about more than the visible, we tend to focus on what we see. In the case of our dogs it's their behavior. We are able to accept that there are some behaviors performed by humans, many which cross the line and are crimes, which if not forgivable, we understand and offer a degree of leniency to the offender. Steal a flat screen TV and you're a thief. Steal food to feed your kids and you may still be a thief but only the hard-hearted (and completely literal) will send you to jail for it. Shoot your spouse to benefit from an insurance policy and not only does the possibility exist that it will become a made-for-TV movie, but here in the U.S. we may kill you for it. Shoot your spouse because they beat you or you stumble upon them in the arms of your best friend, and you may spend your life in jail or not (depending on the skill of your lawyer and the size of your bank account), but a jury of your peers may find it in their hearts and minds to spare you the electric chair (or whatever method of killing people is currently in vogue). We call them 'mitigating circumstances.'

I received an email from a woman with a 100lb dog who would drag her home at the sight of a small dog. The trainer working with the woman suggested she sit with the dog while small dogs passed and ignore her until the dog offered a 'calm behavior' and then reward her for it. The suggestion makes sense when you focus on behavior, but the best part of the suggestion was that the woman sit down, being dragged from a sitting position is probably a wee bit safer than being pulled down while standing.

Imagine being in a room and noticing smoke beginning to pour out of an electrical outlet. Despite your efforts to express your desire to flee, the person you are tied to ignores you. Can anyone blame you if you decide that to save your own hide you need to drag your oblivious companion along with you? Maybe this person knows that smoke routinely comes out of this outlet and has learned that it is irrelevant to both your well beings but you have no way of knowing this. We can teach young humans to; 'say please', 'ask to be excused', 'use your words', but it's not so simple with a dog, especially a dog that believes he's about to become toast.

Even if the woman was able to control the dog, I wondered how long she would be willing to wait for the dog to calm down. Imagine telling a kid that you're going to sit at the table with them until they like broccoli. Get comfortable, you may be there for years.

While being afraid of other dogs and not liking the taste of a particular food are not the same thing, we can work with them in a similar way. First we can acknowledge that a preference exists. The dog does not want to be around other dogs (or whatever they're afraid of) and the kid does not like broccoli. For whatever reason we've decided that both the dog and kid must interact, in a positive manner, with whatever they hope to avoid. We can chop up the broccoli and hide it in pasta sauce, which the kids likes, or smother it with cheese to make it more palatable. This is not that dissimilar to how we can help our dogs feel better about what they currently don't want to deal with. Cut it up into tiny pieces and smother it with cheese. Keep the scary thing far enough away not to matter and add something that the dog likes to the equation. Even if neither dog nor child learns to love what is triggering their reaction, they can learn an appropriate response when faced with it. Little Timmy can learn not to make gagging noises when grandma puts spinach on his plate and Rex can learn not to behave like other dogs are serial killers in disguise.

Getting and rewarding the desired behaviors can work. The challenge for most owners of fearful dogs is recognizing what is a rewardable behavior and making sure that the broccoli is cut up small enough. Many fearful dogs will 'shut down' or offer what looks like a calm behavior, but are displaying what is called 'learned helplessness'. Similarly a dog's behavior can be suppressed and this also can appear to many as 'calmness'. In today's pop dog training jargon it is often called 'calm submission'.

When dealing with a fearful behavior accept that your dog feels passionately about something and then smother it with cheese, a ball toss or a game of tug. And until your dog understands that smoke doesn't always mean there's a fire, take them and leave the room.

PLAY HARD, PLAY FAIR, NOBODY HURT

Posted August 31, 2010

When I got out of college and participated in a year-long outdoor leadership program, playing New Games was all the rage. The motto of New Games is "Play hard, play fair, nobody hurt." Games are designed so that people play with each other, not against each other. There is still plenty of action and consequences for being tagged or caught out, but this usually means your role changes and doesn't mean you can't play anymore. We learned to use them with groups ranging from young children to corporate executives. I was not surprised that one of the games is played by dog trainers to help both trainers and owners to better understand their dogs.

The modeling clay game goes like this: One or two people (the players) leave the room while the rest of the group comes up with a behavior, pose, or action they want the players to perform. When the players return to the room they are given only one piece of information; they are told "yes!" when anything they do is close to what the group has decided they want from them. It seems easy enough until you are one of the players trying to figure out even simple behaviors; stand and raise one foot. There tends to be lots of experimenting with movements and you can watch the wheels turn in players' brains as they try to sort out which behavior is earning them a "yes!"

If you are playing this game and trying to figure out what to do by being told all the things you are doing wrong, it quickly becomes frustrating. Only the most committed players stick with it, shy, timid, or reluctant players rarely get far. What you tend to see is lots of stillness broken up by deliberate movements; raise arm (No!), raise other arm (No!), turn head left (No!). It's not a very fun way to learn and the folks determining correct behaviors soon tire of the game themselves; they want to see the players succeed. It's not unusual for players to give up and stop.

A dog who gives up trying to figure out what their owner wants of them may end up behaving in a more acceptable way (no more trying to get what they want). This is not a big problem if the only thing their owner wants of them is to have them sit down, lie down, or stand still. Indeed most pet owners would be happy if their dogs performed these few behaviors on cue. But the behaviors that get oohs and aahs and compliments of "what a smart dog!" are behaviors which were learned because the dog figured out what was wanted of them, or were shown what they needed to do and were rewarded for it, not because they gave up trying.

Life is easier for dogs when they are able to predict outcomes; not surprisingly, so is our life. Our brains are so good at it that we are not even aware that we are doing it until we suddenly realize that we've been driving and are not sure if we've missed our exit, having been operating on autopilot. Our brains made all the subtle adjustments necessary for staying in our lane and maintaining a reasonable speed, predicting what needed to be done effortlessly. Fearful dogs do better when they can predict what is going to happen next in their world. As obvious as something might be to us, it's not fair and often not correct to assume that it's also obvious to our dogs. Make the unpredictable thing unpleasant, scary, or painful and you up the anxiety level of an already anxious dog. Until the dog is able to learn to predict what precedes the unpleasantness, their overall anxiety can increase. Since life is not a laboratory, what predicts unpleasantness may not end up being the behavior you are focusing on but rather something else in their environment, something you may not be aware of or have control over. Heck it might even end up being you!

Fearful dogs have brains that are very efficient at being scared or feeling bad. Giving a fearful dog ANY reason to be scared or anxious just adds to this proficiency. Training methods that hurt or startle a dog can add to the already overloaded baggage these dogs are carrying around with them. If you're frustrated or not sure how to change your fearful dog's behavior, find a trainer who plays hard, fair, and doesn't hurt.

BE WARY OF THIS CRITICAL M.A.S.S.

Posted October 17, 2010

When I first got out of college I had the good fortune to work for Susan Herman, who, along with her husband at the time, ran a progressive summer camp that also offered summer student-travel programs. I was hired to lead 4-week travel adventures with 12 teenagers and a co-leader. We worked 24/7, organizing and preparing 3 meals a day, driving hours to hiking trails, setting up tents, navigating teen angst and drama, and cajoling 14-year-olds into carrying heavy packs up hills.

During an extensive orientation Susan shared one missive with us that I have never forgotten, "Assume goodwill, no ill will intended." It is all too easy, when confronted by someone's behavior, or the results of that behavior (dirty dishes left in the sink, laundry languishing in the dryer, or a gas tank needle pointing precariously toward empty, for example) to think the worst. How selfish! Lazy! Inconsiderate! When we think this way, our own behavior is affected. We may become angry, short-tempered or frustrated, and it shows.

It's not unusual for dog owners to assume ill will when it comes to challenging behaviors in their dogs. When describing their fearful dog these adjectives are often used: **m**ean, **a**ggressive, **s**tupid, and **s**tubborn. The first time I heard someone describe their fearful dog as stupid I was flabbergasted. Because the dog had not learned *not* to be afraid of things, the owner assumed it was due to a lack of intelligence on their dog's part. Just because public speaking isn't your *thing* doesn't make you an idiot.

Snarling dogs can look mean and aggressive, but, when you understand the underlying emotion, their behavior can be assessed in a very different light. If every time you had politely asked to be left alone and you weren't, should you be faulted for raising your voice? What is viewed as *stubborness* in a dog may be an indication of the lack of skills to perform certain behaviors, or the inability to perform them because fear prevents them. Imagine being labeled stubborn because you refused to lie down amidst a writhing mass of snakes— even non-poisonous ones!

The next time you find yourself upset or frustrated with a dog (or even a human), changing the way you think about their behavior will change the way you behave, and sometimes that's what needs to happen.

FEMINISM & THE ART OF DOG TRAINING

Posted October 25, 2010

If when I was in college someone had suggested that my major of women's studies would help me be a dog trainer, I probably would have thought they were crazy. Majoring in women's studies was like majoring in philosophy or english lit; it made for good late-into-the-night conversations with housemates, but the job market might be thin when it came to hiring someone with a degree in it, as a dog trainer or otherwise.

I will not be the first person to make the correlation between the way women and animals are viewed and treated in our culture. In 1978, *Woman and Nature* written by Susan Griffin included this introduction:

> "These words are written for those of us whose language is not heard, whose words have been stolen or erased, those robbed of language, who are called voiceless or mute, even the earthworms, even the shellfish and the sponges, for those of us who speak our own language…"

She goes on to assemble documentation from textbooks, manuals, and scientific theory detailing attitudes, practices, and beliefs regarding nature and women that have been disseminated over the centuries. They range from silly to barbaric. That masturbation caused blindness may have been distressing news to many teenagers, but that animals do not experience pain in the same way that humans do, and that their shrieking was merely an automatic response, led to practices in animal husbandry that can only be described as obscene.

Theories and edicts can exist to support the status quo and provide excuses for the inhumane treatment of both people and animals. Between god, science, and country there have been no shortage of excuses for inflicting pain and bondage on, as John Muir calls them, "our fellow mortals."

For me, feminism is about discovering the untold stories, the stories of those left voiceless. History is not just about wars and the acquisition of land and wealth; it's about how women, children, and people of color lived, dreamed, and created. It's about art, music, health care, education, and community development. That I might consider what a dog wanted was not an indication of a weakness of character or softness of countenance, but is instead a valuable approach to changing a dog's behavior.

I couldn't help having my BS radar go off when a television personality came up with the explanation that dogs need "pack leaders" to excuse and explain his physical control and intimidation of them. That this was also a man who could explain that women, being what they are, give affection first at the expense of attaining control over a dog, did not surprise me. Women have been blamed for the problems of their children, and the ways we choose to interact with people has often been said to be inferior to the ways of men. What surprised me most was how easily this was swallowed by so many dog owners and trainers.

"Look!" they will say, "See how the dog complies and is cured of their desire to do something of their own choosing." (Women needed husbands, slaves needed owners—how else were they to survive and know how to *behave*?). But it's a benevolent control, they will argue, the dog not only needs it, they want it, it's in their blood. The proof most often heralded, i.e., wolf-pack hierarchy, has been shown to be faulty, yet the belief that dogs live in packs with a defined leader persists. As if without a pack leader, canine or human, all hell will break loose among a group of dogs.

Indeed hell does break loose, but too often it's a hell which we have created and then fault and punish our dogs for struggling to escape from it.

HOW DARE YOU?

Posted November 22, 2010

I often wonder why people are so quick to choose coercion (to force or threaten a dog to comply) as a method for dealing with their dogs. Perhaps they believe that dogs are not smart enough to learn any other way. But I think that one of the main reasons is because their dog's behavior often makes them angry or frustrated.

When I walk a dog on a leash who pulls it really bugs me. I do not like to be dragged along nor do I like to feel like hired help at the other end of the leash— there for the sole purpose of taking the dog outside. When I reach for something on the floor and a dog gives me a hard stare and begins to grumble, I think, "What the heck? My house, my stuff, buddy."

I spend a lot of time thinking about why dogs do the things they do and how to change the things I don't like (along with figuring out how to get them to do things that delight me, such as getting my cocker to rest her head on her front paws on cue). After my initial emotional response of, "How dare you!" I have a list of alternatives I can try to get the dog to comply, or, more accurately, to teach them the appropriate response to me asking them for the marrow bone which is starting to chip and I'd rather was thrown away.

The choice to use compulsion or coercion is often based on the sense of immediacy we feel, which may at times be justified. ("Drop that box of rat poison now!") But more often than not, what we require from our dog does not have a ticking time bomb attached to it. This is especially true with many of our fearful dogs. If a dog must become a socially adept, fearless dog in under 30 days (or whatever time frame has been assigned), I would question the understanding of the basis of fear-based behaviors which the handler has. One of the only regrets I have in regard to the way I handled Sunny was that I was not patient enough, and that I forced him to do things which to this day I can see the negative impact of.

At a Clicker Expo I lingered after a presentation by Ken Ramirez, the head trainer at the Shedd Aquarium in Chicago, to ask him a question. "How," I asked, "Do you get a wild animal to trust you?" He told me that they use a process of counterconditioning and desensitization that starts with only a small amount of exposure to a trainer who is a cause of fear for the animal. No animal is forced to do anything. Why then, I wondered, do we think that we need to use force to work with our dogs who have generations of genetic coding which make them even more likely than a dolphin to want to associate with us?

Now, instead of fuming and saying, "How dare you!" I take a breath and ask, "Why can't you?" when it comes to dealing with changing my dog's behavior. Often the answer I get is, "I don't know how….yet."

ELEMENTARY, MY DEAR WATSON

Posted November 19, 2010

As much of a pain as it was to find myself with a project instead of a pet, I not only adore my fearful dog Sunny (who I am upgrading to my "super cautious" dog Sunny), I am grateful to him for bringing the joy of inquiry back into my life.

As a kid the world was full of endless discoveries and questions: certain types of mud stick very nicely to the soles of your bare feet, peppermint stick and hot fudge make an awesome combination, why is it that if you stand in a doorway with your arms by your sides and push against the door frame hard and long enough when you step away your arms will float up? Adolescence and hormones brought a whole new batch of discoveries (which I will decline listing in case my mother decides to read my blog) and the questions took on a new philosophical bent. It's not that the questions and discoveries cease when we become adults, but the electrifying edge they have seems to dull.

I have always enjoyed being with dogs and training them, but it wasn't until Sunny that I started to find myself experiencing ripples of pure delight when I discovered topics like learning theory and neurochemistry. One of the reasons was because Sunny didn't make anything easy for me. Why wouldn't he come out of the corner? How could I get him to stop being afraid of me? Why was he afraid of me? Might he always be afraid of me? What should I do? Each of these questions pointed me toward something interesting and eye-opening. Sometimes the answers were simple and appealed to my common sense. Other times the answers were neither simple nor constant.

Working with dogs is like being a detective. First I have to figure out, as best as I can, why a dog is doing something. Then I get to think about how to get them to either keep doing it, stop doing it, or do something else. The easy answer can seem to be, just make them.

Years ago I was bequeathed two cocker spaniels. Prior to this I felt no particular preference for the breed. I thought they were too small and cute to count as real dogs. But, as you might imagine, I fell for them. The fact that they need to be groomed and must have their ears, eyes, and lip folds cleaned regularly was certainly not part of what endeared the breed to me, but it came with the package.

When I didn't know much about training, the only solution to performing unpleasant housekeeping on my dogs was to use compulsion—suck it up and deal, little dog. The problem with this was that, not only did I get resistance from the dog, it made the process unpleasant for me, making it less likely that I'd do it, more likely that infections would set in (which caused the cleanings to be painful for the dogs) and made their resistance even more extreme. It became more expensive for me when I brought them to the vet so someone else could make my dog deal with it. This was not a very good system.

Compulsion, bribery, and trickery came with an even higher price. My behavior became suspect. Was a recall being asked for because ears were going to be cleaned? Hands reaching out could be going to grab a collar for restraint, so should be avoided. Even a small head duck offended me. That was not the kind of relationship I wanted to have with any dog, never mind my own.

Then I discovered methods like desensitizing and counterconditioning—rewarding for behaviors I wanted and, even better, getting the dog to be an active participant in whatever the process was. I discovered that, even if my dogs did not enjoy what was being done to them, they could comply with my request for them to hold still while I did it. Even though some procedures require restraint (I'm not sure how to convince Annie that having her anal glands expressed is a necessary evil), I am always pleased when it's over and she shakes it off and then looks at me as if to say, "ok lady not sure why you felt the need to put your finger up my bum, but you did, so how about that liver treat?" Fortunately, most of the things I need my dogs to do don't require me to force them to comply, but, even then, the manner of their compliance is tolerant and accepting, liver treat or not.

Whenever I find myself thinking that the only solution to a dog's behavior problem is to make them do something, I know that I haven't asked enough questions. Sucking it up and dealing should not be the main skill any dog should have to learn, despite the fact that many are masters at it.

Does My Dog Need Prozac?/Debbie Jacobs

CHANGING OUR BRAINS TO HELP
CHANGE OUR DOGS' BRAINS

Posted February 2, 2011

If we can change the way that we think about fear-based behaviors in dogs, the way we handle them will change as well.

It's surprising that there are still people who are unwilling to acknowledge the emotional kaleidoscope that dogs (and other animals) experience. The reality that dogs have emotions is apparent in their behavioral responses, if you know what to look for.

There are trainers who refuse to acknowledge that the emotional stability a dog is able to achieve is not only due to the trainer's handling skills, but is rooted in early development as well. Dogs that are able to positively change their behavior are held up as proof of the validity of certain training techniques, while the dogs that do not improve are labeled to indicate their lack of success; the dog is "too far gone." Pet owners are also held responsible when dominance or flooding-based techniques are not successful.

In a perfect world all dogs would have the opportunity to live a safe and happy life regardless of their emotional and behavioral challenges. In a perfect world we'd work with fearful dogs to increase their confidence by providing them with skills and environments suited to them that allow them to be successful and to flourish and change. In a perfect world we'd all understand that there are edges we can push dogs over that can send them plummeting into the abyss of restraint, aggression, and ultimately death, and then avoid these edges.

"

DON'T FORGET TO BREATHE. BEFORE YOU SAY OR
DO SOMETHING OUT OF FRUSTRATION OR ANGER,
INHALE, HOLD, EXHALE SLOWLY, AND THEN THINK
ABOUT YOUR OPTIONS."

"

WORK WITH THE DOG YOU HAVE

Posted February 28, 2011

I am tempted to say, "work with the dog you have until you have the dog you want." I realize that, not only might it be a bit trite, the outcome of working with the dog you have may not lead to having the dog you want. On the other hand, it might end up that you want the dog you have.

The latter, and a smidgen of the former, has been the case for me. In some instances a dog only needs the opportunity to learn and grow to become the dog of our dreams or expectations. This is true of adolescent dogs who test their owners' patience and training skills. We know from the population of dogs found at shelters that dogs in this age group are often not the dogs their owners wanted.

I was speaking with a trainer friend about a client I was going to meet to help her find ways to work with her fearful, and sometimes aggressive, mastiff. My friend made the point that it may be necessary to "normalize" behaviors for owners in relation to their dog and breed characteristics. In the same way it is *normal* for an adolescent dog to behave like a knuckled-headed brat, it is also normal to have a dog bred for guarding be suspicious of new people or animals entering their territory. It doesn't mean that a dog bred for particular traits cannot learn to be tolerant, flexible, and compliant in relation to those traits, but, in some cases, if the training for this did not begin early in their lives, or fear is added to the mix, it might require an owner to reassess their expectations for the dog.

In my mind I have a picture of what a confident, fearless (but not reckless) dog looks like. I have lived with many. When I watch my dog Sunny I can see behaviors which do not fit with this picture. A dog with the right balance of caution and inquisitiveness will explore their environment. They may startle at novelty but within a short period of time (seconds in most cases) will approach and assess the new object or person. Any overt displays of aggression or wariness should end as soon as the neutrality of the novelty is established. Even after living in our home for over 5 years, Sunny will often avoid or move away from novel objects placed in his environment, objects which other dogs barely notice. However his negative responses to novelty are not as grand as they were and he may also tentatively approach and check out new objects.

I had to normalize Sunny's responses to novelty in my own head. He behaves the way a dog that was not exposed to novelty as a pup, and perhaps one on the more wary end of the genetic spectrum, might behave. As much as I want him to change, I cannot force him to stop being this kind of dog. What I have been able to do is give him skills for dealing with situations that cause his heart to start beating faster (whether it means going to a place he feels safe, or running to find a frisbee and even sitting quietly at the vet).

Sunny makes me work harder than my other dogs when it comes to getting behaviors that I want from him. I don't need to work to get my border collie Finn to be happy and confident with new people. Indeed I have had to work with him to tone down his exuberance when potential frisbee tossers appear on the scene. For years I have lived with Bugsy, an old cocker spaniel, and I admit, with embarrassment and regret, has had almost no training. Bugsy just seems to seamlessly fit into our lives. He's got his quirks but none were enough to warrant effort on my part to change; instead I accommodated them.

I never would have thought I'd want a dog like Sunny but, one evening in a training class watching other owners with their dogs, Sunny gave me the head toss that had tagged along with the click he got for eye contact and I thought, "I wouldn't trade this dog for any of the dogs in this room." Both Sunny and I have been able to change and that's a big part of why I want the dog I have.

OXYGEN AS A TRAINING TOOL

Posted March 15, 2011

I'm an open-minded trainer and dog owner who has looked at and considered the merits of a variety of different training techniques. If a handling or training technique works I am curious to see why it does, or to assess whether what we are seeing in regard to the dog's behavior is actually successful. A dog who has shut-down may have stopped doing something inappropriate, but how's that going to hold up in the long run? If a technique works but there are alternatives which achieve the same end using less force or intimidation, you can probably guess which route I'll take.

Today I heard the darndest thing. While speaking with a group of people, all with professional dog-handling experience of one form or another, I was told about a local trainer's use of strangulation as a tool for achieving compliance in dogs. Several of the handlers had witnessed the technique being used by the trainer and one had been requested by a pet owner to use it on her dog, as she had been taught by this trainer, to get and keep her scared dog on an exam table. The handler deferred. The methods employed by this trainer are self-described as *natural*.

I must have missed the memo referring to the use of oxygen deprivation by animals to achieve compliance in others. Oh wait. I did read something about that; we call it torture.

"

LEARNING IS A PROCESS OF FIGURING OUT
WHAT WORKS AND PREDICTING OUTCOMES.
SOMETIMES A DOG HAS TO GO BACK AND REVIEW!
DON'T BE DISCOURAGED BY WHAT SEEMS
TO BE BACK SLIDING. IF YOU HAVE BEEN
SEEING PROGRESS, STICK WITH A REWARDS-BASED
PLAN. YOUR DOG SHOULD BE ABLE TO REGAIN
WHAT YOU THINK IS LOST GROUND.

"

WE'RE NOT OUT OF THE DARK YET

Posted May 12, 2011

I have been struggling this week with a website a friend shared with me. On the site a "trainer," who seems to boast no qualification other than maybe owning a boxed set of dog training DVDs, proudly describes and documents with chilling videos how a "dominant" dog was put in his place.

The dog, a breed which is known for its wariness and tendency toward hypervigilance, had shown an unwillingness to perform behaviors on cue "unless he feels like it." He has resorted to biting on multiple occasions, including members of his family. The dog's unwillingness to go for walks is ascribed to the dog's desire to be with his "subordinates," i.e., the people he lives with. The dog, supposedly a power-hungry maniac, "whines anxiously" and pees when spoken to in an angry tone of voice; both tactics employed by the stealthiest of confident dogs, apparently. The author deserves an award in fiction because the entire piece is that, fiction. The cause and motivation of the dog's behavior has been made up in order to fit the author's view on dog psychology, that being the desire of dogs to wield power in relationships.

The videos included are painful to watch. The dog appears to have on two collars, some kind of "training" collar and a choke collar, and, in order to balance the playing field, a slip-on muzzle which the dog was forced to wear through 4 hours of coercion and abuse. (Keep in mind that a slip on muzzle, unlike a basket muzzle, does not allow a dog to pant and breathe normally.) Watching a dog fall to the ground to avoid being made to move is wrenching, yet the trainer sees it as one more tactic of a manipulative, dominant dog resisting the will of the true "pack leader." As the dog lies on his side in a last ditch effort to avoid going anywhere, the handler (for I have ceased to be ble to call her a trainer) pulls the dog's tail out from between his legs to "change his energy." Skip the certification for dog trainers; let's require IQ tests as a start.

Finally, after 4 hours of being pulled, dragged and forced to comply, and no videotape left to film in the dark, the dog walks along with the handler.

When someone is caught on videotape abusing a dog, there typically follows a round of petitions calling for the perpetrator's arrest, yet cyberspace is replete with images and videos of dogs being abused and no one bats an eye. They don't bat an eye because the abuse is labeled "training." There was a time when people argued that animals did not feel pain, and this justified and excused the most horrific of treatment. Few would debate that issue today, accepting that dogs have nerves and those nerves register painful stimuli. It is accepted that dogs experience emotions, and one of the most obvious emotions we can observe in dogs is fear. That anyone with a heart, never mind a brain, could subject a fearful dog to hour after hour of torment is beyond me.

I am reminded of Augustine's words, "Since God has spoken to us it is no longer necessary for us to think."

Apparently we are not out of the dark ages just yet.

NOTHING WRONG WITH A DUCK

Posted May 14, 2011

I have found myself being taken to task, chastised, and berated for putting information on my Fearfuldogs.com website that says that not all fearful dogs can be completely *cured*.

Some who label themselves trainers, and others who will not identify themselves at all, have claimed that this is a disservice to people with fearful dogs, that it is not just disheartening, it is wrong. They assert that they have been able to cure all the dogs they have worked with of their fears. One described a process akin to *rebirthing* and offered to take my dog for 6 weeks and return to me a dog that takes treats from my hand and rolls over. I declined. Not only was the price tag of several thousand dollars too steep for my budget, I already had a dog that would take treats and I was not at all interested in a dog that would roll over when approached by a person. In case you weren't aware of it, dogs will roll over to indicate their lack of intention to be confrontational. It is a source of the misinterpreted "alpha roll." It's a way of asking to be left alone. (Not all rollovers are for this reason. Go ahead and give that belly a rub if you know the dog is asking for one.)

What I should have suggested to this person (who refused to give me any information as to who they were) was that I would consider their offer if in 6 weeks they came back to me fluent in a foreign language. Fluent, not just able to order a meal or find a toilet. I say this because the development of language in a human's brain has a sensitive period during that brain's growth when the acquisition of language is most efficient. There is also a sensitive period in a dog's brain development during which the ability to interact with novelty, and the skills to engage socially with people and other dogs, also occurs. Once this period of development is over, it does not mean that a person cannot learn a second or third language or that a dog cannot learn the skills to interact appropriately with novelty, but that some will be better at it than others (and that some will always speak with a funny accent).

I don't want to toss out the baby with the bathwater in regard to their message to me. My goal is most certainly not to discourage people living with fearful dogs. An important piece of the equation is that as we work with the dog, both of us learn new skills. Along with the development of these skills, the challenges we face with our particular dog become easier. In order to learn these skills we need to be grounded in the foundation of how behaviors are built and changed. We need to understand that behaviors can be driven by powerful emotional responses that we should acknowledge and address.

Understanding how a dog's brain develops is important. If you have a duckling and are expecting it to grow up to be a swan, you may be disappointed; but what's so bad about being a duck anyway?

THE PATH OF THE HEART

Posted May 18, 2011

Back when I was in university I attended a class on Carlos Castaneda's books, the Teachings of Don Juan series. Ah, those were the days. For the uninitiated, the books, written as a recounting of Carlos' experience with the shaman Don Juan, are full of magical experiences and lessons for living what some might call an enlightened life. They were, and still are by many, believed to be a non-fictional account of Carlos's adventures, both spiritual and physical, in the deserts of Mexico with his teacher and guide Don Juan.

Written in the late 1960s they were perfect for the introspection and questioning of the status quo of the decade and the age of the readers, i.e., college students faced with the challenges of entering a soul-sucking world. Don Juan was a "facing-your-fear-and-doing-it-anyway" kind of guy. It's not necessarily bad advice, except maybe for teenagers who are contemplating doing something stupid and would be better off listening to what their fear is telling them. But Don Juan was all about potential, and then there was the peyote.

"A warrior is able to advance or retreat from any position," is a saying I've had in my head for years which I attributed to one of the Castaneda's books, but now wonder if perhaps it was Lao Tsu who penned it. I can't find it, so let me know if you do. I like it. I think of it often in regard to fearful dogs. They too need to be able to advance or retreat from any position. Too often the option to retreat is removed. It was Lao Tsu who said, "I would rather retreat a foot than advance an inch." Probably another good one for fearful-dog owners to keep in mind, though I'm not sure what it means in regard to war strategy. We can begin the desensitization and counterconditioning process where the dog has shown us they are most comfortable.

The following quote comes from one of Castaneda's books; it's one of Don Juan's lessons for Carlos.

"Before you embark on any path ask the question: Does this path have a heart? If the answer is no, you will know it, and then you must choose another path. The trouble is nobody asks the question; and when a man finally realizes that he has taken a path without a heart, the path is ready to kill him. At that point very few men can stop to deliberate, and leave the path. A path without a heart is never enjoyable. You have to work hard even to take it. On the other hand, a path with heart is easy; it does not make you work at liking it."

And per usual I think about it in the context of dogs. Dogs who, when given the chance, seem to always choose the path of the heart.

One of the most fulfilling aspects of spending time with dogs has been paying attention to each individual and discovering what path their heart is on and being invited along for the journey.

READY, SET, RESCUE!

Posted May 25, 2011

Recently I ruffled some feathers on an online forum. It was not my intention and I usually try to stay out of most of the networking-site forums because they are often too upsetting, but something moved me and I posted a comment. The original posting was about a 15-year-old girl who had started a rescue group. It was an upbeat, "isn't this heart-warming" post and I could not shake the not-so-heart-warming reaction I was having. Had I realized that the girl was a member of the forum and would read my comment, I probably would not have written a thing, but that's history now.

I tried, apparently without success, to express my unease with celebrating an animal rescue headed by a 15-year-old while supporting her intentions and motivations. I strayed from the, "You go girl!" response and the hits started coming. I was the grumpy lady who needed to worry more about people who weren't doing something to help homeless animals and not about the ones who were. I was wrong to assume that a 15-year-old would not have the skills or abilities to do a good job rescuing animals. I was the naysayer trying to squash the hopes and dreams of a motivated, caring, young human. I felt like Scrooge in December.

I gave it a couple more shots at trying to explain myself and then excused myself from the room, but I was surprised. The forum was specifically about animal rescue and I found it difficult to imagine that no one else shared my concern that, good intentioned as anyone may be, animal rescue is a complicated and challenging task; and as bright and conscientious as this young woman might be, at 15 how much could or should we expect from her?

I am not naive nor so far removed from reality that I expect animal behaviorists and professional trainers to be starting animal rescues in droves, but I do believe that animals deserve that level of skill and expertise when it comes to determining their future. Their lives depend on it. The belief that all they need is "time and love" is so far off the mark for many of them that I cringe when I hear someone involved in rescue say it. That sentiment is naive and removed from reality.

The attitude of many seems to be that, not only can anyone who grew up with a dog and having watched a few seasons of the *The Dog Whisperer* be a dog trainer, anyone can start an animal rescue. Even barring the hoarders and dog traffickers involved in rescue, there is no shortage of well-intentioned people who cause extreme suffering to the animals in their care. The fact that it's unintentional is beside the point. The impact of a "bad" placement extends beyond the immediate dog and family. I have lost count of the people who have told me they will never adopt a dog again because of bad experiences with dogs who needed more than time and love.

At this point, the best I can do is wish this young woman good luck in her endeavor—the dogs are going to need at least that, and more.

DEAL WITH THE DREAD

Posted June 11, 2011

William James, a 19th-century psychologist described his anxiety in this way: "A horrible dread at the pit of my stomach ... .a sense of the insecurity of life."

We cannot know for sure if dogs experience dread, but anyone walking into a vet clinic with a dog who would rather not be there has surely seen what could be described as a dog anticipating something unpleasant, dreading what is to come.

A dog who cowers and resists being put on a leash may not be concerned about the leash itself, but what the leash predicts, i.e., exposure to things or situations the dog is afraid of. When people ask my fearful dog Sunny's name, I may tell them but ask them not to use it. I have also told people his name is Bosco. For a people-fearful dog, being spoken to predicts a social interaction with which the dog is not comfortable. When a dog hears their name they may begin to dread what is going to happen next. In my dog's case, Bosco means nothing to him and, if I suspect someone is not going to be able to follow my instructions regarding not talking to him, if they use Bosco he is less likely to have a negative response to hearing it.

In order to help a dog learn to cope with and even feel good about something, we have to address their fear and concern early on when the dread begins, and then take a step back. A dog's ability to feel comfortable and confident improves as they learn to become proficient at a task or skill. A child will not learn to swim if they are afraid to put their feet in the water, so we start by helping them to learn to do that. As they become proficient at entering the water, we can slowly add to and increase the skills they need in order to swim. A dog who learns to put one foot on a step (or take 2 steps up) an A-frame may cease to dread approaching stairs or an agility obstacle. We allow the dog to practice just this simple behavior, moving away and returning to practice it again.

The challenge for most of us and our dogs is our sense of urgency for successfully completing a behavior. We adopt a dog afraid of moving through hallways, and, because we live in an apartment building, expect that the dog is going to learn to be comfortable immediately. We need them to be comfortable in order to take them outside. We bring home a puppy who has never been left on their own and plop them in a crate for hours at a time, and expect they will quickly discover the joys of solitude because we have to go to work on Monday morning. We would not be foolish enough to assume that just because we're going on holiday to the beach in two weeks that a non-swimmer is going to learn to become proficient enough at swimming so they'll be comfortable and safe in the waves just because WE need them to be.

When dealing with fears and anxiety, follow the chain of experiences back and start by addressing the dread. We can't force skills on a dog, but we can help them to want to learn them.

CRATES: A GOOD THING GONE BAD

Posted June 23, 2011

You might wonder why I am choosing to go on a rant about crates. (This is a warning that a bit of a rant is headed your way.) In an attempt for full disclosure, I have a wire crate with the door closed behind me with a puppy snoozing in it. Crates can help with house-training and transporting dogs. They can keep our houses safe when we aren't around to manage a destructive dog. A crate can provide a refuge for a fearful dog. My crate was providing a place where the pup could chew on a bone without having a bigger, bone-stealing dog bother him.

What I wonder is, when did it become acceptable to confine an animal for most of a day, and why do we think they'd be happy with it? "My dog loves his crate!" you say, and so he should, but it is my contention that the overuse or misuse of crates is contributing to many of the behavioral problems owners and trainers are experiencing. Want a puppy? Be sure you have a crate! Work 12 hours a day? No problem, get a crate! Have a young, developing dog who is exploring his world with his mouth? No worries, get a crate! Need some time to relax and not deal with a dog seeking attention? Stick him in a crate! House-training a puppy and don't want to risk your carpets? Confine her to a crate! The advice isn't all bad, but more of a good thing isn't always helpful.

Young dogs can suffer the most from excessive confinement. While their brains are developing, instead of exploring and learning lessons from the world and other dogs, they are stuck in a crate. One of the most frustrating questions I am asked is how to stop a dog from barking while left alone in a crate, especially when they are left for far too long. Dogs are social animals and being left alone can be scary. I realize that it is flippant and unrealistic in many cases to tell someone that not leaving a dog in a crate is a good way to stop them from barking when they're in it. For example, some people have chosen a dog and do not have the time needed to adequately address its needs, and have a houseful of shoes and table legs they prefer not to have chewed. So now what? Let the punishment begin! Spray the dog, put a bark collar on it, and yell at the dog. It's the beginning of a downward spiral.

As for loving their crates?—I love curling up in my bed with a good book, but not for 16 hours out of 24. I'd especially be unhappy about not being able to do more than just stand up and turn around while I was in it for that much time. If there were other dogs or people in the kitchen or playing games in the living room, I'd probably want out. If I heard a spooky noise coming from the basement, I'd probably want the option to either check it out or get the heck out of the house. To make matters worse, if I had no way of knowing (as young, inexperienced dogs don't) that my confinement was limited, I might begin to become stressed and anxious when I had moments of really wanting OUT and had no idea when or if that was going to happen soon enough for my liking. The alternatives of being tied up outside or left alone in a fenced in yard are not much better and can lead to an array of behavioral problems.

The lack of exposure to novelty is one of the leading causes of fear-based behaviors in dogs. It is during their early months when this exposure is key to the development of a dog's tolerance and resiliency. Puppies who do not have the opportunity to have social interactions with other dogs, children, men with beards, and hats can become fearful or aggressive.

Keep your crate but use it thoughtfully. Plan crate time for when a dog is most likely to appreciate it. Build a dog's comfort with their crate by making it a place of good things, and allow the dog the choice to leave BEFORE they become upset and have bad associations with it. Explore other options; day care, dog walkers, board and train. Most of all, be realistic in your expectations for these fabulous, sensitive creatures we choose to share our lives with and who don't have much choice in the matter themselves.

DESPERATELY SEEKING DISTANCE

Posted August 22, 2011

During a seminar I suggested that people with fearful dogs reward their dogs for moving away from what scares them. Did I mean reward them for trying to flee? For many this flies in the face of what their goal for the dog is. Don't we want to get dogs closer to what scares them? Well, yes, and no.

Working with any dog is a process and throughout that process the dog's behavior changes, at least that's what we're hoping for. But sometimes the changes are not what we'd like. As a fearful dog gains confidence we may see happy, eager to engage behavior toward a trigger. Or we may see a dog who, with some confidence, discovers that they are more willing to be assertive and express what they truly feel, which for some dogs is, GET AWAY FROM ME! It's that "get-away-from-me" behavior that can become dangerous for a dog and whatever they are afraid of.

Unless you know with certainty that a fearful dog is going to end up loving a trigger, you take a risk whenever you encourage them to get closer to it. Early on with Sunny I used to take him for off-leash walks on a wooded trail near town. When people appeared he would run off into the woods sometimes barking. As time went on he became bolder and I remember thinking how much progress he was making when he no longer chose to run off into the woods, but instead followed after people. I also remember having a flash of doubt at what was really going on. Was he truly just investigating them? Was that head lift toward the jacket tied around their waist a sniff or had he tried to get his mouth on it? Because he had never shown any aggressive behavior toward me or my husband, nor had any of the people who had handled him previously mentioned aggression, it was not a consideration I kept in the front of my mind. I do now.

I am not suggesting that we never work with our dogs to increase their comfort level when in closer proximity to their triggers. It's how we go about it that matters. When we remove the option to move away from something scary, a dog may hunker down and suck it up, hating every second of it. Some may be OK with it and figure out that it's not as horrible as they expected it would be, but there will be some who will respond aggressively in order to make the exposure end. Don't ever eliminate "move away" from a dog's repertoire of behavior choices.

Ultimately, our dogs need to learn skills for dealing with what scares them, if only long enough for a vet visit, but how we get them there matters. The ability to decrease proximity between themselves and a trigger is not necessarily proof of success. You may be willing to go into work and pick up your paycheck and still hate your boss, or the work you do. People are not the only animals that can go "postal."

MAY I HAVE THIS DANCE?

Posted September 2, 2011

I was reading a blog recently written by a woman who confessed that, though she had not always been a dog lover, she now had to greet every dog she saw. If that is truly the case, I hope we never cross paths. My dogs don't necessarily want to greet every human they meet. Even my fabulously social and cuter-than-buttons cocker spaniels began to hide under my chair when sitting at an outside cafe in Provincetown because they couldn't take one more person cooing over them. I understand that people's behavior is coming from a place that is essentially good, but it's also often only essentially good for them.

At a large pet event I watched as a dog trainer, who seemed like a lovely, kind person, took the leash from a woman who had brought along a young dog she was fostering. Walking away with the dog, the trainer began to gently manipulate the dog into heeling position and a sit. This was occurring in a function room with high ceilings, hundreds of people, tables, chairs, and even ferrets. I watched as this sweet, stressed dog complied with the requests being made of her. Even if the trainer and dog had met before, it could only have been the equivalent of a first date and here the trainer was asking the dog to hop into bed with him. The dog, to her credit did the best she could.

I was desperately trying to figure out the point of the exercise. Was the trainer trying to impart some skills to the foster caregiver? To the dog? It sure wasn't a teachable moment as far as I could tell. Was the trainer trying to show off his skills? Even if only gently pushing down on a dog's hind end and lifting up their tail to get it to sit works, I was far more impressed with the dog than the trainer. It was loud enough in the room that I had to lean closer to people speaking to me to hear them, and crowded enough that people brushed by as they maneuvered past. I can't imagine what the dog, with senses more sensitive than my own, was experiencing. But I tried. I tried to imagine the world at that moment from the dog's perspective. A dog who had not only never been in a place like this before, was also a dog in transition.

The experience likely did not cause any damage to this resilient and tolerant dog, but I continued to wonder why two people who were obviously caring, kind, gentle dog lovers would take the risk of putting a dog into a situation in which she might be continuously pushed toward being overwhelmed. The only conclusion I could come to was that they were unaware of what the dog was trying to say. I'd like to think they'd care, if they had taken a moment to pay attention to what the dog was asking for with her slight resistance, look-aways, attempts at avoidance, or, in one case, flopping to the ground.

Fortunately, most dogs are resilient and adaptable. They manage to learn and cope despite how we handle them, not because of how we handle them. Some of that handling may even contribute to their ability to cope with extremes, but some dogs may not benefit and become anxious or react negatively. If we really and truly love and care about dogs, why don't more of us inquire as to whether a dog would like to add us to their dance card or sit this one out before we drag them onto the dance floor?

LOSING GROUND WITH FEARFUL DOGS

Posted September 7, 2011

As a member of an online group which addresses fearful dogs, I routinely see questions by others about what to do when their dog regresses. Your dog is doing great and then suddenly, seemingly with no cause, they revert to an old behavior you have struggled with replacing. Look around and you'll see shattered dreams and dashed hopes scattered all around.

Imagine watching a toddler who after getting the hang of taking a few steps plops down on their diapered behind and hearing her parents groan, "Darn it, I thought for sure she knew how to walk." If they can get past their disappointment and see her through childhood, let's hope each skinned knee isn't met with the same concern.

Change is a process. We humans can be an impatient bunch. We want stuff fast and we want it our way. Not being satisfied with baby steps, we can push too hard and topple the kid over. Walk, goddammit!

Learning never ends. Unless it's an indication of conditions which hinder the ability to walk in general, it's not the falling on your butt that's the problem. The problem is not wanting to get up and try again. Dogs can appear to regress and still be moving in the right direction so long as they are willing to keep trying.

Behavior will change as conditions change. If our shoes pinch our feet we may not be happy about walking. It would be too bad if someone labeled us as lazy instead of understanding we are trying to avoid a blister.

It may not be obvious to us, but when we see changes in our dog's behavior, there are usually other things going on. Respect their decision to choose a different response and, even if you never figure out what is causing it, at least acknowledge that your dog does have a reason for their behavior and your lack of insight or understanding about what it is does not indicate a shortcoming on their part or yours!

If you handle a fearful dog with kindness and respect, helping them maintain a feeling of safety and building skills, the chances are good that if she does slide down the slope a bit, she will have the skills to regain the ground that seems like it was lost. The view from the summit is still glorious however long it takes to get there.

JUNK FOOD ISN'T CHEAPER & PUNISHMENT ISN'T FASTER

Posted September 26, 2011

An article in the *New York Times Week in Review* section compared the costs of fast food vs. home-prepared meals. There were some who argued that the challenge of getting people to stop eating fast food was the cost; because it's less expensive, it makes sense that people will choose it, except that it isn't less expensive. It isn't less expensive at the outset, i.e., in the actual dollars spent to purchase the food, nor is it less expensive down the road when the cumulative effects of high fat, high sodium, and low fiber begin to exact their cost to our health. The cost of meals we make ourselves is in time and the energy required to purchase and prepare it. Some would insist that it is this lack of time in our modern-day schedules that promotes trips to the drive-thru, until you look at the numbers of hours we spend watching TV, updating our Facebook status, and, lord knows, writing blog posts.

Quoted in the article is Dr. David Kessler, former commissioner of the FDA and author of *The End of Overeating*. Dr. Kessler's book is a must-read for anyone battling a food addiction, and an important read for dog trainers as well. The first part of the book details studies done with animals to determine how behavior is affected by reinforcement. They were the studies that helped trainers understand how the delivery and quality of reinforcement impacts whether or not a behavior is repeated consistently or not, or if the behavior is maintained. The reinforcement used in the studies was food.

Take a peek into any training chat group or forum and you will witness the continuing battle being waged about whether or not it is wise, effective, ethical, or faster to use punishment to get behaviors from our dogs. Punishment, by definition, decreases the likelihood of a behavior being repeated, but for many trainers and pet owners punishment is used to attempt to increase a behavior, that behavior being something other than the behavior they have punished the dog for performing. It's a backward approach that works often enough for people to keep using it. Knee Fido in the chest when he jumps on you and it's likely he'll stop jumping and do something else. If he's lucky that *something else* behavior is one you approve of or else Fido will be subjected to yet another form of punishment until, if he's willing to keep trying (and let's face it, dogs don't have much choice in the matter if they want to keep being fed), he finally comes up with something that passes muster.

This may not be a big deal for some dogs but for others it may be. There are costs to be considered when choosing to use punishment. There are the up-front costs—the cost to the relationship between the dog and handler, the cost to the dog's sense of safety, or the cost to the dog's willingness to engage in the dance we call training. Then there are the down-the-road costs; suppress a behavior and you may find other equally as distasteful behaviors cropping up in its place.

In the article the author poses the question about our behavior in regard to the consumption of junk food: How do you change a culture? Dr. Kessler's response was this:

"Once I look at what I'm eating and realize it's not food, and I ask, 'what am I doing here?' that's the start. It's not about whether I think it's good for me, it's about changing how I feel. And we change how people feel by changing the environment."

This change will lead to healthier and less costly food consumption habits. I am going to take this and stretch it a bit. Let me rephrase his statement this way:

"Once I look at what I'm doing and realize it's not training, and I ask, 'what am I doing here?' that's the start. It's not about whether I think it's good for the dog, it's about changing how they feel. And we change how dogs feel by changing the environment."*

We change their environment by removing the risk of being forced, intimidated, scared, or hurt. We ensure they always feel safe and that making the right choice is easier than making the wrong one. It may not always seem easy to do, but, in the long run, it's the healthiest choice to make. Fearful dogs live with more stress than is good for them, no reason to supersize it.

Apologies to Dr. Kessler. Hope he doesn't mind.

Posted October 26, 2011

In Costa Rica there is a saying, "Poco a poco la hormiga se come el coco." (Bit by bit, the ant eats the coconut.) I use it often in relation to my fearful dog Sunny.

In November Sunny will have been with us for 6 years. He's not the same dog he was when he first arrived, but no one would have any trouble identifying him as fearful of people, unless they only watched him interact with me or someone tossing a frisbee. Sunny is also easily startled by a book sitting outdoors on a table, its pages flipping in the wind; a drawer opening or closing; plates settling in a dish rack; the sudden movement of a rocking chair—all cause him to duck his head, pull his ears back, and RUN AWAY! But, bit by bit, I have noticed changes in his behavior. It used to be that Sunny could not stay in the same room with me while I folded laundry (fortunately for him I'm not big on folding laundry, so its not a daily occurrence); each article of clothing pulled from the basket was a source of concern and, early on, horror (not a statement on my fashion sense!).

Lately I've noticed he's less worried. The past few weeks he's been spending more time in the kitchen/living room area with me and other dogs as I prepare their meals. Sudden changes in his environment will still cause him to startle, but often he doesn't run away. He's routinely coming inside the house through a door that he avoided, instead of heading to his usual entrance around the house via the deck. That he came in through that door when my husband was home was worth noting. After 6 years Sunny remains afraid of him inside the house.

Over the years I've had people, some well-intentioned, others not so much, offer me advice or criticism, inferring or outright blaming me for Sunny's behavior. Early on I had my doubts; was I doing the right thing by Sunny? But years of living with him, studying behavior, brains, and, most specifically, fear, I harbor fewer doubts that the recommendations I had been given were wrong. Most included some form of *make him*—make him walk with you,

125

make him follow you around the house, make him be near your husband. I assume that this technique worked for the suppliers of the advice, but whether they are unable to accurately read their dogs and so are misinterpreting the results, or were handling a dog without the same depth of a problem as my dog, I don't know. What I do know is that my dog did not have the skills or ability to deal with the things that scared him and come out better for it. For six years I have worked on giving him those skills and, as his trust in me has increased (I've become predictable to him), I've been able to "ask" him to do things that he might not have chosen to do on his own, but together with me, he's successful.

Dogs do not ever *forget* that something scared them. It doesn't make any sense to forget that something was once perceived as dangerous. That rustling in the grass may not have been a lion this time, but the animal that gets to breed probably doesn't ever become *laissez-faire* about it. Even if no physical harm ever comes to a dog, the emotional response of fear to a trigger is real, i.e., enough evidence that something is dangerous. We often talk about trusting our gut when we're not sure about how to respond to something. Dogs trust their guts.

This doesn't mean we can't change a dog's behavior—we can—but it takes time and patience. The rate at which a dog is able to change will be unique to them and their particular blend of biology and experience. As our dogs learn new skills and behaviors, so do we. We are also nibbling away at that coconut as we learn about being better trainers, and then bite off another chunk that teaches us something about compassion.

OUR SUFFERING MAY BE THE SAME

Posted November 8, 2011

Years ago when my husband worked at a Boys & Girls Club, he came home one evening and shared his day with me. The adventure began when one of the kids attending an after-school arts and crafts program became upset and shut herself inside a locker. The little girl, living with her mother and brothers in a hotel room to escape from an abusive father, was 6 or 7 years old. Her peaches and cream complexion was framed by long, wavy, light-brown hair, the kind often seen in Raphaelite paintings of young women.

What happened to send this young girl, crying and using curse words that would embarrass a sailor, into the locker was unclear. What we know about children who suffer from trauma or abuse is that it doesn't take much to set them off. They're the kids who haul off and slug someone for bumping into them by accident in the corridor at school. When my husband approached the locker and spoke to the little girl he was met by a barrage of cursing to which he replied, "Wow, those are some big words for a little girl. Want to go get a snack?" Her response was to come out of the locker, sniffling and nodding her head in agreement. Together they went and sat at a table, ate a snack, and talked a bit about how she might try to respond differently next time to whatever affront she felt she suffered.

Later during a staff meeting he was met with criticism about how he handled the situation. He had *rewarded* the little girl for her bad behavior and had provided no punishment. When he told me this story, the wife in me sided with him immediately; he had worked with kids for over 2 decades and had good reflexes when it came to getting behaviors he needed from them. The dog trainer in me went on to explain why he had made exactly the right decision to do what he had done.

It is not hard to understand why this little girl would be suffering emotionally. Even if her response to not being able to have the color crayon she wanted seemed exaggerated to her instructor, this was a kid without a lot of extra resources when it came to tolerance and coping. Her response, however overblown it appeared, was a reflection of her distressed emotional state. Punishing, or threatening to punish her, was not likely to ease this distress. Attempting to reason with her, and get her to acknowledge the error of her ways while she was crouched in a dark locker, would also likely to have been unsuccessful. We don't think very well when we're upset. Distracting her and using whatever means possible to calm her down, in this case the offer of food, diffused the situation, stopped the swearing, and helped her *think* about the situation.

I don't know whether her swearing and locker-hiding persisted into the future. When I first started my journey of thinking about how to help fearful dogs, I was given a paper to read on the effects of childhood trauma and abuse on behavior and physiology. It was apparent that though differing in specific responses, the behaviors we see in fearful dogs are not unlike those of these children. The parts of our brain that process fear are the same, so it is not unreasonable to make the assumption that a dog experiences the emotions associated with fear in ways very similar to, if not exactly the same as, the way we do.

As upsetting, scary, or frustrating a fearful dog's behavior may be to us, it's important to remember that they are suffering. If they could they too might say a few things that would make a sailor blush.

LIVING IN THE MOMENT

Posted November 22, 2011

Of all of the silly things I hear in regard to dog behavior, the proclamation that "dogs live in the moment" takes the cake. It is usually used to criticize owners for being understanding of their dog's past and that, unlike humans, their past doesn't affect them. They are supposedly furry Zen masters of "be here now." The idea that it is the owner's response to their dog's fearfulness or reactivity that is the cause of a dog's behavioral problem, not the animal's history, is an uninformed one.

I'm going to back pedal here for a moment because certainly an owner's response to their dog can and does effect their dog's behavior, but to lead people to believe that the events, or lack of them, in a dog's life have no impact on their current behavior is wrong. It makes no sense for an animal to simply *forget* about things that they felt threatened by in the past. If that was the case, then training, whether using rewards or punishment, would be a waste of time; what they learned today wouldn't matter tomorrow.

Whether a dog is consciously thinking about a scary past event, or is responding based on how they were classically conditioned to respond, may remain a mystery to us as we work with our dogs. Though our dogs may not be worrying about the security of a bone they buried last week (or they might be!), they may be concerned about something that scared them last year. The more potent the emotional charge an event has for a dog, the more likely it will be remembered, consciously or unconsciously, and matter; And that *we* know something is safe or inconsequential doesn't matter. There are plenty of people who are deathly afraid of things that have never harmed them or even have the potential to harm them.

Handlers do need to be aware that a dog's behavior may be affected by their response to a situation, but they should never downplay the effect prior experiences can have on a dog's ability to cope in the moment.

"

THE NEXT TIME SOMEONE TELLS YOU
THAT ALL DOGS LEARN DIFFERENTLY, CRY FOUL!
WE ALL, FROM BACTERIA ON UP, LEARN
FROM THE INTERPLAY BETWEEN OUR ACTIONS AND
OUR ENVIRONMENT. IF OUR BEHAVIOR ACHIEVES
AN OUTCOME WE LIKE, WE'RE MORE LIKELY
TO BEHAVE THAT WAY AGAIN IN THE FUTURE.
IF WE DON'T LIKE THE OUTCOME, WE'RE LESS
LIKELY TO BEHAVE THAT WAY AGAIN.

WE HAVE A CHOICE WHEN WE TEACH OUR DOGS
NEW SKILLS. WE CAN EITHER HELP THEM LEARN TO
BEHAVE IN WAYS THAT BRING ABOUT OUTCOMES
WE BOTH ARE HAPPY WITH, OR USE PUNISHMENT. A
TRAINER WHO TRIES TO TELL YOU THAT "ALL DOGS
LEARN DIFFERENTLY" IN ORDER TO JUSTIFY THEIR
USE OF "BALANCED" METHODS MAY BE UNAWARE
THAT THEY LACK THE SKILLS TO GET THE BEHAVIORS
YOU WANT WITHOUT RESORTING TO PUNISHMENT.

GOOD TRAINERS ARE USUALLY INCREDIBLY
"IMBALANCED" IN THAT THEY RARELY HAVE
TO USE POSITIVE PUNISHMENT
TO TEACH DOGS NEW SKILLS.

"

It's true, sh*t happens, and when it does it's good to know about it. It's like those fast food restaurants with the sign in the bathroom that says, "Please let us know if this restroom does not meet our high standards for cleanliness." If sh*t happens and you don't know about it, how can you clean it up?

In the industry of animal rescue (and find fault with my use of the term "industry" if you like), there is a lot of sh*t going on that doesn't make it into the reports and stories created to provide PR and donations for the group doing the rescue.

I catch sh*t from people who insist that getting a dog into a home and out of a shelter is worth doing, whether there has been adequate evaluation of the dog's and future owner's needs and skills or not. Some will say that the odds are better for the animal—100% chance of dying in a shelter vs. some unknown percent chance of suffering in a home, or wherever they end up. But make no mistake, in plenty of cases they die anyway. They may suffer emotionally and physically while being passed from home to home or shelter to shelter. They may be forced to live a life of confinement or isolation. They may be "adopted" by dog traffickers who sell dogs to labs or fight rings. If the dog is intact, they may be used for breeding. They may end up as part of a hoarder's collection and receive inadequate care. They may flee from their home and never be recovered.

How many shelters and rescue groups have statistics regarding the number of animals still in their original home, with contented owners, a year after being adopted? And if they don't have them, why not? How can we raise our pom-poms and cheer for dogs being placed in homes if those placements are ultimately unsuccessful? How can a group learn to improve their assessment of dogs and potential owners unless they track the results of their current practices and procedures? I already know all of the excuses for not doing this kind of follow-up—time and money being high on the list—but I just don't buy them. If we seriously want to declare ourselves animal advocates then the "out of sight, out of mind" rationale doesn't hold water.

If we are committed to the animals in our care, we can find ways to ensure that we are doing the best we can for them. But we'll never know how to do that until we are willing to expand our vision to include the big picture and not just the snapshot "feel good" moment of adoption.

KEEPING TRACK OF DOGS

Posted December 12, 2011

I wish I had a dollar for every recently adopted or foster dog who goes missing. If I did I'd spend it on one of the new GPS tracking devices available to pet owners.

A day doesn't go by without seeing notices of these lost dogs on my Facebook or twitter feeds. I've had it happen myself and the sinking gut feeling of knowing a dog you have been caring for and care about is out running scared (a potential victim to cars, weather, starvation or predators) is an emotional response I can do without.

People who adopt a dog, especially one with any fearfulness, often do not understand the flight risk their dog poses. Either they are not having it impressed on them by the people organizing the adoption, or they are ignoring the warning. It may be a case of bad luck and timing. A door is opened and a fearful dog, who has been looking for opportunities to escape, does. Or something startles a dog and once they're on the run, they are difficult or impossible to get control of.

Having ID on a dog is a no-brainer. If an unidentified dog is found, it's likely going to end up at an animal shelter and what happens then will vary. Some shelters will make efforts to locate the dog's owner, while at others the dog enters the queue of dogs who will be euthanized if not claimed or adopted within a set period of time. Unfortunately even identification is no guarantee that a dog will be returned to its owners. When my dog who had been living with my mother ran off, I visited the local pound and found her. I would have gone there days earlier except that my mother had called the facility and been told that no dog matching her description was there. My dog also had up-to-date town license tags on her collar.

All my dogs have an ID tag on their collars with my name and contact information on it. Should a good Samaritan find my dog they can contact me directly, perhaps sparing my dog a stay at the shelter. An injured dog with an

ID tag is more likely to receive timely medical care, because a vet can contact the owner to approve what might be costly procedures.

Technology will continue to improve and one day I hope that all dogs go to their new homes with a tracking device on them. In the meantime, we can help our fearful dogs so that not only are they kept safe and secure, but we can create a positive, trusting relationship with them so they are less inclined to run away from us should opportunity knock and leave a gate open.

THE PROBLEM WITH PACKS

Posted December 13, 2011

Of all of the misconceptions about dog behavior we are faced with, the idea that dogs are pack animals is among the stickiest.

Yes, dogs are closely related to the grey wolf, a species which does form cohesive and lasting packs when in the wild, packs which function to ensure the continuation of the genes of the animals in that pack. They hunt together and raise their young together. Stray or feral dogs may form groups, may scavenge together, may even have best buddies, but they do not establish packs in the same way wolves do. The process of domestication has created a unique beast—an animal far more successful numbers-wise than their close relative, the wolf. Without a doubt dogs are social animals—and incredible ones, at that—and are able to extend their sociability to include us. But this "based-on-wolf pack" idea, although questioned, studied, and disputed for years, remains.

The point of this post is not to argue against the word pack to describe groups of dogs, but rather to invite you to come up with other ways of describing our relationship with dogs. "Pack leader" rolls off the tongue so easily, as opposed to "orchestrator of activities for a fluid grouping of social animals." Even if someone's idea of leadership includes the kinder, gentler kind, the smudge of *alpha* is carried along with it for many pet owners. It becomes apparent in the manner in which owners and trainers handle and interact with dogs. Sometimes its effect is benign but often it is not and we see all manner of inappropriate behaviors in response.

For my own purpose of thinking about my relationship with my dogs, I envision myself as a camp counselor. I am responsible for their welfare, direct their daily activities, mediate social interactions, and teach them how to weave pot holders. Well, we're not quite up to pot holders yet.

"

IF YOU SMELL SMOKE YOU DON'T SIT AND HOPE IT GOES AWAY; YOU DON'T WAIT FOR THE HOUSE TO BURST INTO FLAMES BEFORE YOU START TAKING ACTION. WHEN YOU START SMELLING SMOKE AND NOTICING BEHAVIORS IN YOUR DOG THAT YOU WOULD DEFINE AS FEARFUL OR AGGRESSIVE, DO NOT WAIT AND HOPE IT WILL GO AWAY. FIND A TRAINER WELL VERSED IN REWARD-BASED TRAINING METHODS TO SHOW YOU HOW TO GET THE BEHAVIORS YOU WANT/NEED AND KEEP YOUR DOG FEELING SAFE IN THE PROCESS.

"

CREATING WELL-BEHAVED MONSTERS

Posted December 26, 2011

Years ago I suggested that my sister let her two Miniature Pinschers off leash as we headed off for a walk in the woods near her home. Ooops, my bad. I'd been walking dogs off leash since I was a kid. It never occurred to me that someone's dog would not just go for a short walkabout on their own, but would not come home at all! I've learned a lot since then.

When I was younger and would head off for a walk through the woods and cranberry bogs in southern Massachusetts, my mother would remind me to take the dog. This was when boogeymen were rare and a mother could relax knowing that the family's fat fox terrier was protecting her child.

Nowadays when I head out for walks with dogs, my own or other people's pets, I often carry a variety of kibble, dried liver, chunks of cheese, or chicken. I've never found it to be a burden. Anytime a dog looks at me, comes to me, or stops and waits for me, the chances are good they'll receive a treat. I do most of my training on these dog walks.

Because of my lifestyle and expectations for my dogs I don't worry about getting most behaviors "under stimulus control." This means a dog only performs a behavior when asked for it. You don't want a dog going into the obedience ring deciding to sit or down to take a load off when they feel like it, but in my life it doesn't matter. I want my dogs to look at me, trot back to me, walk jauntily by my side, and wait for me without having to ask for those behaviors. And they do. A lot. That's the monster part, sometimes I just want them to go about their business while I go about mine.

Most days on our walks I want to think grand thoughts, talk to myself, to come up with ideas for blog posts, etc., but there they are—a dog or two or three walking along next to me in position for a nice loose leash were they to have one on. To them it's a game and they want to play it. They wander off and come racing back and look at me as though we were long-lost friends. I have to shoo them away—go on, explore, sniff, be distracted! Surely there's a chipmunk out there that needs harassing.

It's my own damn fault and I know it. If you consistently reward a dog for a behavior, the behavior gets stronger. If you reward a behavior intermittently, it becomes less likely to go away. Do the former for awhile and then switch to the later and you've really gone and done it. I don't always give my dogs food when they look at me or come back to me. Sometimes I tell them what absolutely amazing dogs they are or nod and smile and give them a wave to get back to the business of sniffing out wildlife poop and preferably NOT rolling in it.

I guess I have to live with the check-in monsters I've created. As for my sister's dogs, we found them, eventually.

IS GETTING ANOTHER DOG HELPFUL FOR A FEARFUL DOG?

Posted January 1, 2012

It's not uncommon for people who are living with a dog who is afraid of people or new environments to wonder if getting another dog would be helpful. It's a generous thought, I'll give it that, but there are many potential pitfalls to take into consideration before making that leap.

Being around others that a dog feels safe with and trusts can help lower stress levels. This is why comforting a dog who is afraid can be so beneficial. With lowered stress, some fearful dogs are able to do things they might not be able or willing to do on their own. If we like the things they are able to do, it makes sense that we'd consider providing them with that benefit all the time by adding a dog to our household.

Here are the questions I'd ask anyone considering getting a dog to help their fearful dog:

• Why, if the dog you brought home felt more comfortable being around other dogs, did you adopt him to begin with if you didn't already have another dog in the house?

• Unless you deliberately set out to adopt a dog with fear-based behavior challenges, what makes you think that you, the breeder, rescue group, or shelter is going to do a better job a second time around at finding an appropriate dog for you who not only has to be a good pet but also needs to rise to the occasion and be a stellar role model and companion for a fearful dog?

• Are you willing to hire a professional trainer or behaviorist to help you find an appropriate dog to add to your household?

• Are you prepared to spend more time training and more money for the upkeep of an additional dog?

• What will you do if it doesn't work out as you'd hoped?

It's a lovely thought that a fearful dog will see another dog interacting with people, other dogs, novel objects, etc., and learn to do so happily themselves. I could watch a dozen people jump out of a plane and still be reluctant to fling myself out the hatch. There are people who won't taste a new food even though an entire group of people consumes it routinely, but we expect dogs to do better than this? What if instead the new dog learns to be more wary and cautious of things by following the lead of the fearful dog?

Pairing a friendly dog with a fearful dog for the benefits of social buffering and modeling can end up backfiring. I don't worry when my border collie Finn races up to people to greet them. His behavior may be considered rude but the worst that is likely to happen is that someone will end up with paw prints on their pants. He likes people and sees every human as a potential frisbee tosser. Sunny, on the other hand, would be better off not being drawn toward people by following Finn's example. He's not comfortable with people and getting closer to them can end up scaring him. This could lead to an aggressive response.

Unless I have complete control over Finn's behavior, being able to stop him in his tracks as he heads off to greet someone, I run the risk of having Sunny join him. Finn's arousal is benign, Sunny's is not. Annie, my adult cocker spaniel displays her "greeting disorder" anytime a new person or dog appears on the scene. She is harmless, annoying but harmless, but her reactivity is not helpful when I am trying to train a fearful dog to stay right where he is. In trainer speak we call this *proofing a behavior*, and means that we practice a cue, such as "wait" over and over in many different situations with a variety of distractions in order for the dog to gain the skill to perform the behavior wherever, whenever we ask for it, regardless of what is going on around them. It takes time and effort. Sunny has a solid "wait" in many situations, but he is affected by the arousal level of other dogs, and this makes getting him to wait more challenging.

This is often when people will suggest the use of some kind of powerful punishment to teach the dog that moving is not an option. I will not go into it in depth in this post but the risk of *contextual conditioning* is real. Anything that the dog experiences along with the punishment can become associated with the negative experience, including the thing they already are not feeling good about. To this day I am not inclined to eat cherry snow cones because as a kid I caught a stomach bug and the last thing I ate prior to being sick was a cherry snow cone. The snow cone itself did not cause the vomiting but was associated with it.

To trust that a dog will not harm something, we need to be certain that they are no longer afraid of it. Better that they love it but, short of that, a dog is less likely to bite something they do not feel threatened by. There are no magic-bullet cures for fearfulness in dogs. The benefits of social buffering are real, but the tasks of training and using behavior modification are ours. We need to get our understanding of dog behavior and training polished up before we expect another dog to *fix* our fearful dog.

"

IT'S NOT UNUSUAL FOR ME TO HAVE NO IDEA
WHAT SOMEONE IS TALKING ABOUT, EVEN
WHEN THEY ARE USING EASY-TO-UNDERSTAND
ENGLISH; THEY MIGHT HAVE GOOD CAUSE
TO THINK THAT I'M STUPID.

DOGS DO A DARN GOOD JOB OF FIGURING
US OUT, MOST OF THE TIME. THE STRESS
OF BEING SCARED, YELLED AT, OR PUNISHED
IS NOT LIKELY TO HELP WHEN THEY CAN'T.

"

Posted January 3, 2012

When we have a dog who is afraid of people we often focus on getting the dog to move closer to them. What we should be focusing on is encouraging the dog to do whatever makes them feel more comfortable around us. If whenever I stand up, lean, or move toward a dog and that dog moves away, I will put the moving away behavior on cue (a verbal or visual signal that prompts the dog to perform a specific behavior). The behavior is actually already on cue, my movement is a signal to the dog to get away from me, so I change the cue. This can be helpful when we have a fearful dog living in our home with us.

To change a cue is a simple process, present the new cue then the old cue. With enough repetition the dog learns that the new cue predicts the old cue and begins to respond to the new cue as soon as it is presented. In the case of training a behavior like "sit" we can eventually drop the old cue. This is a fun activity to do with any dog and how trainers come up with cute tricks. Instead of saying "sit" they hold up a sign with the word "sit" on it and the dog appears to be able to read. With fearful dogs the old cues may never be faded, we may continue to stand up out of chairs or walk in a dog's direction, but they can lose their potency for causing a fearful response.

Let's say when you take a step toward a dog she skitters away (keep in mind that moving away can also be a polite response from a dog who is not afraid). The dog may be startled or experiences fear by your movement and goes to a place where they feel less afraid. By helping a dog learn to predict your movements you can lower the level of fear they experience. I use a hand gesture and say, "Go on." What you choose to do or say is less important than being consistent with it. You can also use a treat tossed away from you to prompt the behavior and put distance between the two of you before you move. The hand movement of tossing a treat can morph into the cue.

After giving the new cue, I move. In time the dog learns to move away from me before I take a step toward them. When I do move they are already in a place they feel safer and don't experience the same hit of fear they did before when I moved and they were closer to me. At this point I can toss them a treat or ignore them. By cuing the dog to get some distance before I move, I am removing a startling, scary experience which is associated with me. With enough practice this causes two important things to occur: First, they learn they will be forewarned before something scary is about to happen, which helps to lower stress and anxiety, and second, their response to me moving is no longer based on fear; the dog will position themselves in the place they need to be for the desensitization and counterconditioning process to continue.

In time the dog may choose not to move as far away, or not move at all. When a treat has been added to the mix, moving away becomes a positive experience for the dog and is no longer colored by fear. Eventually, we may find that if we don't cue the behavior and simply move toward the dog, they no longer have a negative response at all because all our movement ever predicted was that a treat would be tossed to them.

DANCING IS **NOT** ALLOWED

Posted January 17, 2012

Early in our relationship my husband, an avid tennis player, hoped that I too might learn to enjoy the game. I knew that the chances of that were slim to none, but needed to at least give it a try. My attitude is that if someone really wants to play with me they'd hit the balls to me, rather than try to make me miss them. I quickly realized during the one time I played a game of tennis with my husband that the sooner I hit all the balls over the fence and out of the court the sooner I could leave and get on with things, like a walk with the dogs. My husband continues to play tennis, just not with me.

We give a lot of lip service to having a good relationship with our dogs but I wonder if our dogs could talk, what they would have to say about what is really going on between us. Few pet owners would say they have a bad relationship with their dog, but if questioned about it, it's often challenging to find something good about it, from the dog's imagined point of view anyway. Sure the food may be welcome and having a safe, comfortable place to sleep is nice, but that should be a given in any relationship a human has with a domesticated animal.

I live with a border collie and sheep are out of the question, and I do feel sorry about this for his sake, so I try to find other activities which make his eyes sparkle. As with most dogs what it takes isn't much. A few minutes tossing frisbees, some stones splashing into the river, an off-leash run and anything I can think to ask him to do in exchange for a few bits of cheese may not make up for the lack of sheep, but I have tried to look at our relationship from his side of things.

Imagine that you LOVE to dance and you partner up with someone who not only doesn't enjoy dancing but is adamant about preventing you from ever dancing again. How's that for a good relationship? Now imagine your partner was to say that if you really loved them you'd be happy not to dance, that your life should be complete without the music, without the movement. How long before the bloom is off of that rose?

"

DON'T WORRY ABOUT REWARDING A SCARED DOG
WHO IS BEHAVING INAPPROPRIATELY. YOU
WOULDN'T WAIT FOR SOMEONE WHO WAS
DROWNING TO STOP SCREAMING BEFORE YOU
PULLED THEM OUT OF THE WATER.

"

MINIMUM DAILY REQUIREMENTS

Posted January 31, 2012

When my fearful dog Sunny (or if you are troubled by the labeling of dogs, my dog with extreme fear-based behavior challenges Sunny) first came to live with us, I had dreams for him. In the summer we'd go to South Pond and people would toss frisbees and balls for him to swim after, we'd take long hikes in the woods with friends, or anywhere we'd go he'd get to join us. I imagined that as soon as he could get himself out of the corner all the pieces would fall into place and we could get on with pursuing my dreams for him.

As time went on the reality of the dog I was living with began to settle in. I set my sights on more mundane activities such as helping him go out of the house without a panicked dash and to come back in without having to be caught and encouraged back in on a leash. Being able to get all 55 pounds of himself in and out of the car on his own took precedence over my South Pond dreams. It did happen to be at South Pond where Sunny hopped into the car on his own for the first time, but it was because the voices of people, traveling over the water from a beach on the other side of the pond, scared him so much he sought out the security of his spot on the floor behind the passenger seat.

We attended a variety of training classes including agility and obedience. Sunny even went through a mock obedience trial where he "stood for exam." But who was I kidding? I had no interest in entering him in any events and his ability to barely tolerate the classes was as far from how I want my dogs to feel when spending time with me as you could get. Getting himself out of the corner of the living room was a big step for Sunny, much bigger than I had imagined it would be, but it was a step, not a leap.

Today I am content to have a dog who is housebroken, can go in and out of doorways, comes on cue, gets in an out of the car on his own, stays with me (most of the time) during walks in the woods, can be handled by a vet, loves finding dogs to play with, and can enter a training facility and be excited to chase tennis balls I lob against the wall. I have lowered my expectations for my dog with extreme fear-based behavior challenges, but I've never stopped dreaming of the fun he might be able to have, someday.

THE STOCKHOLM SYNDROME

I was reading a post in a crossover trainer's blog and was struck by the implications of this comment made about her observation of Cesar Millan at his Dog Psychology Center.

"…He walked in with me and one could definitely sense he had an effect on the dogs. I concede he does have "something" about him that effects the dogs."

I am not sure why there is an implied apology in conceding he has an effect on dogs. There is no doubt he does and the Orwellian irony of what it is seems lost on many, including him, with his talk about "unstable" pack leaders.

Dogs, even dogs with behavioral challenges, are not stupid. Many are hypervigilant and extra sensitive to anything they perceive threatens their safety. Anyone, man or beast, who comes into their environment is immediately assessed for their potential threat to the dog's safety. Even if a particular dog was not physically restrained, alpha rolled, choked, shocked, or poked (all main techniques of Mr. Millan's *rehabilitation* repertoire), they will respond to his *presence* and the reaction of those dogs who have been *dominated* by him. It's not unlike sitting on a subway and having a young thug get on the car, giving you one of those "I WILL kick your ass bitch" stares. They too will have an effect on the pack of riders.

The Stockholm Syndrome is a real and well-documented psychological response to fearing for your life. One need not even be submitted to constant abuse in order to give up trying to fight or flee. Random threats of violence are enough to keep kidnap victims sitting in cars while their abductor runs into the gas station for a cup of coffee. Some victims even fall in love with their captors. Take away a dog's control—an easy thing to do with choke chains, muzzles, shocks, and prongs—and it's easy to get the same kind of compliance.

A dog subjected to repeated acts of *dominance* by their handler, acts which likely seem as random and unreasonable as those portrayed in movies by the bad guy who pistol whips the hero for looking at his shoelaces, can also be adversely affected by this treatment. That Cesar Millan repeatedly misreads signals and cues from dogs is no secret. That he and trainers of his ilk manage to convince pet owners that their mythologies of dog *psychology* are accurate and justify their abusive treatment—the more upset and needing special attention the dog, the more abused they are—is no surprise. But I will leave it to the therapists to determine if there is a form of pathology in it and our willingness to watch and pay for it.

One day when our consciousness evolves there may be a tribunal and people who abuse animals in the name of training or rehabilitation will be called to task for it; seats should be saved for the TV producers who seek these people out to make a profit off of the recorded and televised abuse of dogs